SOCIAL
Holiness
THE COMPANY WE KEEP

JONATHAN S. RAYMOND

ALDERSGATE
PRESS

The Salvation Army Crest Books

Endorsements for Jonathan S. Raymond's

SOCIAL HOLINESS
THE COMPANY WE KEEP

• • •

Goethe said, "Tell me with whom you associate, and I will tell you who you are." Raymond illuminates this truism from biblical and personal perspectives, and with temporal and eternal consequences. With solid biblical exegesis and practical life illustrations, the author heeds Solomon's counsel, "Walk with the wise and become wise, for a companion of fools suffers harm" (Proverbs 13:20).

Commissioner William W. Francis,
retired Salvation Army Territorial Commander (Canada)
and Chairman of the International Doctrine Council

Dr. Jonathan Raymond has made a significant contribution to Wesleyan Holiness literature with this book. By placing the life of holiness within social relationships, it helps us see how our lives should be led in community.

Allen Satterlee, The Salvation Army
USA National Literary Secretary

We indeed are shaped by the relationships we place ourselves in, principally with a holy God and those who keep company with Him. Be prepared to see your walk with Christ in relational terms as Raymond issues an invitation to the divine dance in fellowship with our Holy God.

Kevin Mannoia, Founder and President,
Wesleyan Holiness Connection

Here is a unique and relevant perspective on Christian formation and the pursuit of holiness. Dr. Raymond explores the biblical and theological significance of the communal setting, the "ecology" of faith experience and development. Bereft of community, faith may be ingrown, stunted and self-serving. We are called to revel in the enrichment, discipline, and sanctifying grace the surrounding faith community can afford believers who prayerfully choose the "company they keep."

General Paul and Commissioner Kay Rader
of The Salvation Army

We are reminded in these pages how important are the influences of others in helping us understand the pure and perfect love of God. Raymond helps us deepen our understanding of social holiness and allow God (the "Potter") to continue shaping our lives in community. We grow in holiness as we inspire and help others to also serve suffering humanity to the glory of God.

Oscar P. Sanchez, Commissioner,
Territorial Commander, Mexico

There are only a few great books today on Christian living based on Wesleyan theology. This new book is one. The author masterfully contrasts modern Western individualistic thinking to that of Wesley's. The emphasis is on holiness that comes through the work of the Holy Spirit that uses family, other people, groups, educational systems, and other social environments to bring about the personal best in God's children. A must read for every Wesleyan student.

Dave Hudson, Commissioner,
National Commander of The Salvation Army

Having been shaped too much by individualistic Western culture, Wesleyans are finally rediscovering that John Wesley was right: "there is no holiness but social holiness." Jonathan Raymond is uniquely gifted to help us understand why by unfolding the social dimensions of human nature and how profoundly they are bound up with growth in holiness.

Stephen A. Seamands, Professor of Christian Doctrine,
Asbury Theological Seminary

Jonathan Raymond reminds us of the need for the full message of the gospel and that we must practice holiness by walking with others this journey of life. This is a much-needed message for all who are seeking a deeper walk with Christ and a life of holiness.

Carla Sunberg, General Superintendent,
Church of the Nazarene

Social Holiness is important both theologically and practically. Raymond's compelling and personal commitment to Christ intersects with a deep conviction for faithful witness to others. This treatise on social holiness is timely in an increasingly self-absorbed and polarized citizenry.

Sandra Gray, President,
Asbury University

Dr. Raymond reminds us that becoming more like God happens only as we embrace the gift (and at times the crucible) of real relationships with serious Christ-followers. Iron never becomes sharp in a vacuum, but only through intentional, substantial, regular contact with other iron.

Daryl A. Diddle, Senior Pastor,
Wilmore Free Methodist Church, Kentucky

This is a semi-autobiographical reflection on the journey of holiness. It comes from a developmental perspective and is full of classic references from the Wesleyan tradition. We resonate with the assertion of social holiness, abiding and growing in Christ together. With Christ, we are working together toward "the healing of all creation." Praise God!

Alison and Ian Campbell,
The Salvation Army – Integrated Mission

In helping readers better understand "social holiness," Raymond engages "the divine, intimate ecology of holiness." Christian spirituality in the Wesleyan/Salvationist tradition is not only personal and private but also much about others. Preachers and small group leaders will do well to draw on this engaging and articulate volume.

General Shaw Clifton,
Eighteenth General of The Salvation Army

The author is a skilled writer and trained social psychologist. The result is an invaluable book integrating social psychology and theology – highlighting the social and communal nature of the doctrine of holiness, something so often emphasized in the Bible but forgotten when holiness is applied only to the life of the individual believer.

Roger J. Green, Professor Emeritus of
Biblical and Theological Studies, Gordon College

• • •

SOCIAL HOLINESS
THE COMPANY WE KEEP
By Jonathan S. Raymond

PUBLISHED BY:

ALDERSGATE **PRESS**

The publications arm of

HOLINESSANDUNITY.ORG

IN COLLABORATION WITH:

The Salvation Army Crest Books

SANATIONALPUBLICATIONS.ORG

Publication Design
& Management:

lamppostpublishers.com

Printed in the United States of America

Soft Cover ISBN 13:   978-1-60039-310-5
ebook ISBN-13:   978-1-60039-982-4

Library of Congress Control Number: 2018931582

Dedicated to

Lyell M. Rader Jr.

Exemplar and Ambassador of Holiness

ACKNOWLEDGMENTS

Giving birth to a book is like actually bringing new life into the world. It is a labor of love over many months if not years, and it is not a solitary exercise. It takes a village. The voices of others whisper between the lines and their fingerprints may be found on the shape of the book's clay. In short, to acknowledge that the book is occasioned by the influence and contributions of several persons noted below is to leave out many others from whom I ask forgiveness.

I keep the company of someone who's been my best friend for nearly fifty years since courting in college. Irene is God's lifelong blessing. Over the years I've taken on many of Irene's best characteristics and qualities. That's what happens. It's a cliché, but we really do become the company we keep.

This certainly can be said of the influence of my undergraduate professor and his wife, Dr. Alan and Yvonne Moulton (Asbury University). In them the theory (theology) of holiness has come alive. They have been real, walking, breathing, heart-beating saints, disciplined in their spiritual journeys, engaging means of grace in their own lives, and still encouraging others along the way. Their lives illumine what holiness looks like. The more I've been in their presence, the more their lives shape mine. They radiate God's presence. Their interest and investment in my life express God's compassion and grace. Through them God's hands shaped the clay of my life over years. God the Potter still uses them as a potter's wheel, instrumental to his creative touch.

The shaping of my life in Christ's likeness (holiness) is a social/ spiritual process and outcome. God deploys others as formative blessings and means of His continuing, inexhaustible grace: close friends. They include mentors and key authors. The company of authors in particular includes the writings of present and past saints, like Samuel Logan Brengle, Frederick Coutts, E. Stanley Jones, Dallas Willard, and more recently Lyell M. Rader, Jr., Diane Leclerc, Howard Snyder, Timothy Tennent, J. D. Walt, and others.

These are the company I keep and the wheel upon which the Potter shapes the clay. That's how social holiness works in and through the company we keep, alive or not, in the flesh or in print. The whisper of their voices may be heard in the reflections of this book.

Thanks Be to God

I give thanks to God for dear friends in whose company God's presence is real and palpable: Lt. Col. Lyell Rader, Jr., to whom this work is dedicated, Dr. Alan and Yvonne Moulton, mentors in holiness; Dr. Roger Green, lifelong friend and co-editor of *Word & Deed*; Commissioners Dr. William and Marilyn Francis, life-long friends and exemplars; General (Dr.) Paul and Commissioner (Dr.) Kay Rader; Dave and Fawn Imboden; Dr. Kevin Mannoia; Dr. Barry L. Callen; Lt. Col. Allen Satterlee; Dr. Michael Peterson; Dr. Howard Snyder; Aaron David Raymond; Dr. Jerry M. Michael;

and Dr. C. Everett Koop, with others whose mentoring and prayer lives continue to refine my understanding of social holiness. I hold an unspeakably grateful heart for those, living and passed on, whose lives and writings have been inspirational in ministering to me along the way.

In writing this book, I've drawn from the theological roots of my Salvation Army life and upbringing, my exposures to friendships and mentors in the broader Wesleyan-Holiness tradition, and my formal training in the social-behavioral sciences. It's my hope that plumbing the reflective depths of social holiness will add to the "knowledge that surpasses knowledge" (Ephesians 3:19), not only for Salvationists but equally for brothers and sisters in Wesleyan-Holiness heritage denominations, universities, seminaries, colleges, and beyond. Glory to God!

CONTENTS

FOREWORD

I welcome this timely book on social holiness for several reasons. First, and most importantly, God the Trinity lives in unending communion of Father, Son, and Holy Spirit, and God invites us to "become participants of the divine nature" (1 Peter 1:4 NRSV), which is at once holy and social.

The book is indeed about *social* holiness. It uses that term the way John Wesley did, as referring to what holiness *essentially is*, not to the potential impacts of holiness in society. Holiness most thoroughly and profoundly affects society as it is grounded in Christlike community.

There is no better way to holiness and happiness, Wesley emphasized, than being in close relationship with God and with others who are on the same journey. This book's subtitle—*The Company We Keep*—underscores this point. As Dr. Raymond writes, "Other persons are God's means of pouring grace into our lives." And again, "God uses the company we keep and the company we provide as the divine means of grace along the way of holiness."

This approach of Raymond is thoroughly biblical and immensely practical. Such holiness also involves *accountability*, the author appropriately points out. Christian holiness immerses us in accountable community as God shapes us into people who exhibit the mind of Christ.

Emphasizing that genuine Christian holiness involves all our social networks, this author speaks of "the ecology of holiness"—the ways God works to bring wholeness and healing in our relationships with one another and with the whole creation.

These chapters are clearly written and expressed. The author helpfully weaves his own spiritual pilgrimage into the narrative, adding interest and a sense of practical realism. Given these strengths, the book will be a help to people who truly seek to love God with heart, soul, strength, and mind, and their neighbors as themselves.

Dr. Howard A. Snyder, author of *The Problem of Wineskins,*
Community of the King, and *Salvation Means Creation Healed,*
former professor of the history and theology
of mission at Asbury Theological Seminary.

PREFACE

The mission of Methodism in the heart of John Wesley was "to spread scriptural holiness across the land."[1] What he meant by scriptural holiness may surprise many persons who think of holiness as only a personal and private matter. John Wesley is often quoted (paraphrased actually) as saying, "All holiness is social holiness." What he said exactly was, "The gospel of Christ knows no religion but social; no holiness but social holiness."[2]

This book is about social holiness. It is written broadly, not only for friends in the Wesleyan Holiness tradition, but in particular for friends in my own faith community, The Salvation Army, and for all who hunger for God's best, holiness and righteousness. It's a work guided by reflections on the company we keep.

All company of others brings consequences. The central premise of my writing is that we become the company we keep and, if so, then let us keep company with those who keep close company with Christ. Let us first seek directly the company of Christ and then also seek it through the company of others who dwell each day in Christ.

The focus on social holiness stands in contrast to the volumes of writing on holiness from a perspective that is heavily Western and individualistic. It is difficult to find a treatment of the subject that is not strictly personal. In reflection over a lifetime, I've come to the conclusion that Wesley's take on holiness is true. It is more than a personal experience. My own history is rife with the fingerprints of others who've been instrumental as parents, teachers, mentors, authors, and friends in my own journey.

More than the social contexts of spiritual influence and understanding of others, it's clear to me that the very essence of holiness is found in the social and moral nature of God as Trinity. The essence of God is holy love shared between and among the Father, Son, and Holy Spirit. By divine revelation, we know the persons of the Trinitarian God to be co-equal in power and glory, and mutual in unity and love. Together, the three persons of the Trinity are a perfect circle of fellowship open to all humanity as we remain open to intimacy with God in unity and love.

Icon of the Holy Trinity, Andrei Rublev, circa 1425.
See the full color image on the inside front cover.

In the fifteenth century (1425), a Russian monk by the name of Andrei Rublev created the *Icon of the Holy Trinity*.[3] Some refer to it as the icon of icons. Inspired by the Genesis 18 passage, this icon depicts the visit of three angelic persons eating the meal provided by Abram and Sarah. At the time, one visitor announced to them the future birth of their son, Isaac. The three visitors around the table may be understood to be God in three persons, the holy Trinity.

In Rublev's work there are three primary colors. They illustrate the essence of the one God in three persons. The garb of the Father is in gold signifying perfection, fullness, and the source of life. The God in Christ, the human, is portrayed in the color blue signifying sea and sky. Christ is taking on the world and in particular humanity. His hand is holding out two fingers, together representing within both spirit and matter. Finally, Rublev uses the color green in the apparel of the Spirit to convey fertility, fecundity, blossom and bloom, divine and eternal life. The three persons are gazing at each other in intimate expressions of love, and each one's hand is pointing at the others. It is a picture of perfect, holy love, unity, and divine fellowship.

While the symbolism of color is inspiring, what is most significant is how they are portrayed together in their positioning and fellowship. They encircle a shared space around a small table. On the front of the table is a small, empty rectangle. Art historians mention the finding of glue residue on the original icon suggesting that at one time there may have been a mirror glued to the front of the table.

A mirror in an icon is quite unusual. Catholic Franciscan mystic Father Richard Rohr interprets the icon as suggesting that God is not a distant, static monarch. Instead, the three persons in divine fellowship are in what early Fathers of the church called *perichoresis* (the root word in Greek for choreography). In other words, the persons of the divine Trinity are in a divine dance. The mirror represents our seeing ourselves in the dance with God at the table of fellowship.

The icon is an invitation to enter socially and spiritually into the divine, intimate ecology of holiness. The mirror represents seeing ourselves restored to the image of God, present at the banquet table, and participants in the divine nature. The table is not reserved for the Three, nor is the circle closed, but open to all. Rublev's icon occasions reflection on the divine, inclusive, perfect love of God expressed in the intimate, social nature of the Trinity, opened in all its fullness as a dance, a banquet table, a social ecology of holiness, and the eternal company we may keep.

This is also a book that juxtaposes Wesleyan theology with social psychology. At the heart of both we find matters that are relational. While theology is about truth found in Scripture as revelation, social psychology represents truth discovered through the science of human behavior and social, relational contexts. The matter of social holiness is discussed through a synthesis of the two approaches to truth and understanding.

God often is revealed through others. Through others God speaks to our hearts and lives. Others convey divine grace and loving kindness and reach us deep down in our very being. By means of others, God shapes us spiritually into His likeness. God does the same in others' lives through us. God as Trinity is essentially relational and interpersonal. The good news is that, with all of humanity in mind, God's love continues to be poured out in undeserved grace. Perfect love draws us into a divine circle of unity and fellowship.

This book is about social holiness, the how and what of the inner life of God in us and through us to others. It is about God's ultimate purpose. Glory to God!

Jonathan S. Raymond
Wilmore, Kentucky
January, 2018

SOCIAL
Holiness
THE COMPANY WE KEEP

one

ON THE ONE HAND, AND ON THE OTHER

...no holiness, but social holiness.

John Wesley

...together with all the saints...

Ephesians 3:18

L ook back and you will see that we pass through perpetual exposures to others, often in small, influential groups and settings. That's my experience. Over the years, God used a diversity of socially spiritual contexts of family, church, education, and work to form the character of my soul. It is also my experience that God uses us to reach out to others in social holiness. This book is about how God uses social ecologies of holiness, the company we keep, to His glory!

I was born into a family that was highly relational. I am the third son in a line of five brothers and a sister. Our parents were officers (ordained clergy) in The Salvation Army. This meant that we were thoroughly Wesleyan in word and deed and destined to be Salvationists. We were immersed and nurtured in Wesleyan doctrine and a life of service to others. As children we learned that God is relational, a social being. How God could be one God and yet three persons, God the Father, Son, and Holy Spirit, was confusing then and still remains a mystery.

By the time we were three or four, we knew that "God is love" (1 John 4:8) and loved even me. We were nurtured in the Wesleyan spirit that reflects the relational thought, heart, and lives of John and Charles Wesley, and also those of William and Catherine Booth. We were formed spiritually and socially within a Wesleyan worldview that sees life as essentially relational.

As children we learned early that God is a social being of perfect, holy love. As teenagers, we came to understand that God made us socially and morally like Himself (Genesis 1:26-27). We discovered not only that God's nature is holy love, but that His presence is everywhere. In our home our parents cultivated an awareness of God's presence in reading the Bible and prayer at the beginning of the day. They called it the "half hour of power." Around the dinner table we finished the evening meal with scripture reading and prayer.

The family was the primary social setting of our spiritual formation. But so were other social, spiritual contexts: Sunday school, worship, summer camp, VBS, teen fellowship, Wednesday night prayer meetings, five years of Salvationist catechism called "corps cadets," initiatives that reached out to others in love, especially to the poor, and a litany of other exposures, mostly through the social context of the church. Along the way we became acquainted with God largely through the faithful love and help of parents, teachers, mentors, exemplars, and friends. Looking back, it is easy to see how God used many others to influence us in our youthful life together and in our spiritual development as part of a faith community.

We also learned about the fallen nature of humanity and accepted as truth the idea that the sinful world in which men and women are born included us. Nevertheless, God's plan continues to work for the world's salvation from sin and death and for our full salvation, our reconciliation with God and restoration to purity of heart and life, perfect love, and intimacy of relationship with God made possible by God's grace that comes through others. While growing up, for us the "others" were parents, pastors (officers), lay leaders, youth leaders, Sunday school teachers, camp counselors, brothers, other friends, then college professors, roommates, and authors. A diversity of ordinary people over a lifetime comprised sanctified, social contexts that offered the living water of God's salvation.

Going Forward

Going forward, well beyond those earlier formative years, I now appreciate how God uses the exposures to and encounters with others to nurture holiness. The experience of God's love, through the faithfulness of those I now consider saints, spiritually formed my life in holiness and righteousness.

God is a worker and puts us to work. As we are transformed by grace, God uses us to reach out to others in love and fellowship. His grace is not only for us, but to flow through us. God does not work through interpersonal transactions as if grace were a commodity to be exchanged, Rather, by love God saves and transforms sinners into Spirit-filled, Christ-like people. While God can do this work alone, He calls us and others to partner with him in reaching out to others in love. God does this by giving ordinary people major roles and responsibilities, influencing others in his work of redemption and restoration.

This is one way of describing John Wesley's sustained and passionate concern for the restoration of God's moral image manifested in holy love and purity of heart toward God and all humanity. We see this in the social/spiritual contexts in which Wesley was prompted to "spread scriptural holiness throughout the land." This is the nature of social holiness. It is the holy love of God reaching out to others, transforming hearts and lives to the praise of His glory.

Be Holy as I am Holy

We read God's words to the people of Israel, "You must be holy because I, the LORD, am holy" (Leviticus 20:26). God was ending the Israelites forty-year journey through the desert and preparing them to enter the Promised Land. The land would be holy because it would be occupied by a holy people in whom God himself would take up residence.

In the New Testament, we read this: "Just as he who called you is holy, be holy in all you do; for it is written: 'Be holy for I am holy'" (1 Peter 1:15-16). In the new, post-Pentecost community of faith, God would take up residence again as the Holy Spirit. The Apostle Peter was writing to the early church scattered throughout the Mediterranean world of his time. The listening audiences who heard these texts were not just a collection of individuals. Rather, God was addressing people in the faith community, a nation in the Old Testament and the followers of Jesus, the early church reported in the New Testament. In both cases, they were to be a light to the nations.

In the case of Peter's directive to be holy, he was writing to the church as a whole with a desire that the people would let the light of their holy lives shine in such a way that the world would see their good works and glorify the Father (Matthew 5:14). God's great desire then, as it is now, was for the church members to collectively live lives of holiness together. God's vision for their destiny was clear. Together in the social, moral context of community life, they would shine together as a people of holiness. As then, God's focus for us remains social holiness, holiness of heart and life in sanctified, socially spiritual contexts of profound love for God and love for others. All this is within the larger desire that together we realize our part in God's will being done on earth as it is in heaven.

The Wesleyan Spirit: No Holiness but Social Holiness

This discussion of social holiness is written in the Wesleyan spirit. It engages Wesleyan thought regarding the way of full salvation (*via salutis*) made possible by God's grace through the company we keep in Christ. It is about the social dynamic of God's nature at work in our collective fellowship and in our spiritual formation together as faith communities. It proclaims the fullness of life in Christ by the Holy Spirit in and through the company people keep.

The Wesleyan idea of full salvation is captured in three points of understanding: (1) salvation is not merely a rational assent to the truth of a proposition, based on faith responsive to God's grace, a trust in the merits of Christ's life, death, and resurrection. It is faith that our sins are forgiven and we are reconciled in our relationship with God. This is not by our own personal work or merit, but by faith through God's grace; (2) salvation is more than forgiveness of sin. It is also spiritual transformation whereby we are inwardly renewed by the Holy Spirit who shares witnesses with our spirit an assurance of our salvation, and makes possible an infilling of holy love that is of God; and (3) holiness is not just personal for individuals, but a social reality for whole communities of faith and for society as well.

In light of this third point, John Wesley is well known for what is actually an imprecise comment: there is no holiness but social holiness.[4] This is often said to give recognition or credibility to the importance of socio-economic activism, social transformation, social services, social welfare, and social policies, none of which John Wesley directly meant in the first place. He was interested in God's grace active in the social development of character, the socially spiritual support of others, and the accountability to others necessary to our spiritual formation and holiness.

No Solitary Matter

Two quotes from John Wesley underscore a broader, holistic, social understanding of salvation. Wesley was critical of the misplaced idea that holiness is a solitary, individualistic, private matter. He stated that in the gospel of Christ, solitary religion is not to be found. "Holy solitaries is a phrase no more consistent with the gospel than holy adulterers. The gospel of Christ knows of no religion but social, *no holiness but social holiness.*"[5]

Wesley later preached, "Christianity is essentially social religion…to turn it into a solitary religion is indeed to destroy it…. I mean not only that it cannot subsist so well, but that it cannot subsist at all…without living and conversing with other men." His brother Charles is said to have added that such social engagement was God's way to "nourish us with social grace."

Typically, holiness writers discuss holiness from a Western cultural context of individualism. They focus on an interior, personal experience, emphasizing piety and personal relationships with God. While important, few move beyond the Western habit and inclination to view holiness only as personal and to be seen through a cultural lens of individualism. This book provides another perspective and thus is more aligned with Wesley.

Viewing holiness with the cultural assumption that it is only personal can be myopic and introspective. When it comes to understanding holiness, we tend to assume that it is a matter of private aspiration or achievement. However, the gospel comes and is passed on, not as an object like a baton in a relay race. It is a holy relationship with God to be passed on to others. It originates from God's work in us and then through us.

As holiness is passed on, it is not only about you or me. It is about loving God in obedience, and loving others, reaching out to them with a desire for holiness that is for them. Holy love is bigger, wider, higher, and deeper than something merely personal and private. It penetrates the deepest recesses of the human heart, rises to the highest heaven, and reaches out to the farthest heart and soul. It is how we are impacted, influenced, and shaped by others and the Other, God, and how we reach, impact, and influence others in Jesus' name.

Holiness is the social, ecological reflection of the values and virtues of the Kingdom of God. It is observed in our obedience to Christ's great commandment. It calls us to engage in compelling, dynamic, spiritually social, and therefore interpersonal relationships in loving God, others, and ourselves. We need not, should not remain myopic, introspective, or preoccupied with self. Even when seemingly personal, all holiness is always social holiness. Holiness is a relational treasure trove of God's grace. Glory to God!

Holiness as Essence

Serious Christians know that before there ever was creation there was the Creator whose essence is holy love. God was, is, and always will be both one and three. God is Father, Son, and Holy Spirit, undivided in essence, perfect in unity and harmony, of one heart, mind, and will. The Bible makes clear that we are made in God's image for a social, dynamic, interactive life with God as the Trinity. It is the good news that God invites us together into the Trinitarian life of fellowship. It's an invitation to be intimately acquainted with

God. In such shared intimacy, we become participants together in God's social and moral nature (2 Peter 1:4).

Holiness is not a private matter. In the language of Old English, we read God's words, "Be ye holy." They were directed toward all of Israel. The "ye" is like saying "y'all" in the American south. "Y'all be holy." This is the case throughout Scripture. God is giving direction to a people, to a relational plurality, to all the saints. It is more than direction. It is a gift of the divine essence, God's nature and very self-given to the community of faith, the church, which the Apostle Paul referred to as "the Body of Christ" (Romans 12:5, 1 Corinthians 12:12-27, Ephesians 3:6 and 5:23, Colossians 1:18 and 1:24). The idea of social holiness is that the "Body" reaches out and shares the essence of God, holy love, with others.

Holiness and Social Influence

I was trained at the doctoral level to do research in social psychology. This is the science that gives special attention to how we view and affect each other, how people think, influence, and relate. It's about relationships, how we make sense of the world and are shaped in the dynamic, interpersonal interaction of self with others.

For instance, while there are physical measures of things like weight, height, and body temperature, there are realities that cannot be so measured. Our observations and assessments of others and their assessments of us are less tangible, but nevertheless real and reflected in the phenomena that social psychologists study: attitudes, behavior, beliefs, values, self-concepts and self-esteem, self-perception and self-control, consensus, persuasion, conformity and obedience, prejudice, discrimination, hostility and aggression, moral judgments and attributions, moral intuition, attraction and intimacy, liking and loving, altruism and helping, conflict and peacemaking.

So much of what captures the interest of social psychologists may be found in Scripture. The Bible speaks about the social, interpersonal realities of life and the influence we have on others and that others have on us. This includes the matter of social influence and holiness. In the Sermon on the Mount, Jesus proclaimed to the crowd, "Let your light so shine that others may see your good works and glorify the Father" (Matthew 5:16). That was not a one-on-one, private, confidential whisper out of hearing distance from everyone else. It was a proclamation to a crowd gathered on a hillside, spoken in a strong voice to the masses.

We can also assume that in using the five words "Let your light so shine," the "so" was in reference to holiness. Jesus was saying, "Don't keep your light of holy love in the dark, y'all. Let it shine in the company of others, in holiness, so that y'all bring glory to God." In the company we keep, holiness, as the essence of holy love, is social in its influence on others and of others' influence on us. The company of others becomes the means by which God works in our hearts through others and in the hearts and minds of others through us.

We are social creatures whose personhoods, values, worldviews, habits, attitudes, dispositions, moral judgments, ethics, and quirks are shaped by the influence of others. The company we keep is the human agency through which God comes alongside, reveals His nature, and provides the way and means to know him, serve him, and know ourselves. While holiness is personal, it is not private or solitary. In the company of God, the nature of holiness is social. Holy love has a source and a destiny, and holiness is a gift of God's holy love strengthened by the Spirit through the company we keep.

In the course of a lifetime, we may keep company with many others in hundreds of settings. Life's journey, as mine has been, includes many stops along the way with transforming immersions in several particularly influential, social/spiritual contexts.

It is the Holy-Spirit-filled essence of those social/spiritual contexts that make possible God's influence on us and through us as God reaches out in social holiness and becomes the company we keep.

DISCUSSION QUESTIONS

1. In what ways would you say that your family, church, friendships, school, or work experiences have shaped the way you think about holiness?

2. When you think of holiness, who comes to your mind? Why?

3. How did Jesus' own life display holiness, especially in relationships?

4. Jesus said (Matthew 7:16), "By their fruit you shall know them." Have you seen others socially and spiritually relating with one another in ways that reflected social holiness?

5. How has the company of others impacted your life along your journey?

6. How is the essence of social holiness becoming real in your relationships?

two

HOLINESS CLARITY

*When the Spirit of truth comes, he will guide you
into all truth.... He will bring glory to me by taking
from what is mine and making it known to you.*

John 16:13-14

O ccasionally the worldwide news turns its spotlight on the matter of holiness. On September 4, 2016, Pope Francis officially declared the "dispenser of mercy," Mother Teresa of Calcutta, the church's newest saint. His action brought a diversity of responses ranging from delight to confusion and criticism. Some thought it was an appropriate honor. Others criticized the Pope, saying it was too soon or there was not enough justification.

How should we think of sainthood? What is it and what does it mean to be holy or a saint? My own impression is that most people are confused. Like the two despairing disciples on the road to Emmaus, there appears to be real confusion about God, the gospel, who Jesus is, and what salvation means. This seems the case inside and outside the church. It's not difficult to encounter broad-based confusion about what is meant by holiness. The need for clarity is apparent both in and out of Christian circles, and confusion has consequences.

Where there is confusion there is frustration, division, derision, and failure to reap the benefits of clarity. Without a clear understanding it is difficult to move forward with God's intended best. With a lack of clarity we are prone to wander. We lack a spiritual GPS. We often don't know why we are frustrated.

For some, the lack of clarity and frustration occasions dismissal. When the idea of holiness comes up, some would rather not be bothered. They avoid thinking and talking about it. For others, a lack of clarity provokes division and tensions in the church at large and between denominational positions on holiness, even within a single congregation. The lack of clarity causes confusion. It occasions derision and disparagement. It results in the snuffing out any remaining embers of the "fire of the Spirit" in us when we could be a blazing fire.

The problem is a lack of clarity on the "what" of holiness that occasions confusion and consternation and results in our abandonment of any pursuit of holiness. For many people, a Trinitarian understanding of God is missing. For believers and non-believers, God exists on the margins of understanding, a being that exists somewhere in the shadows. Where there is clarity, it's on Christ Jesus, the cross, and an empty tomb. An intellectual conception of God is haphazardly packaged into an opaque, propositional belief in God with little effort to take one's understanding farther.

Often the Holy Spirit is left out of the picture, with little understanding of the continuing work of Jesus Christ by the Holy Spirit in and through the church to the world. This is because the "what" of holiness is poorly taught and preached by those with little enthusiasm, clarity, and personal experience themselves.

The confusion about holiness is often due to superficially held concepts and less than rigorous reading of Scripture. Scripture clearly lays out God's desire that we be holy. It makes clear the way forward in holiness, the nature of holiness, and examples of holy living. We find biblical truth about holiness from Genesis to Revelation. Ignoring an abundance of Scriptural guidance and revelation, we find our pursuit of holiness stifled. It leads to ingrained misunderstandings. Such misconceptions yield dismissals and dysfunctional dogma unwelcoming to holiness.

What Holiness Is Not

The most common confusion is that holiness is undesirable. People too often assume holiness to be either an unattractive form of elitism or legalism: elitism because it is thought to be only for the holiest, the few saints who separate themselves from all others and aspire to be "holier" than others, sanctified snobs; legalistic, because holiness is assumed to be an exercise in bondage to the long list of do's and don'ts enforced without mercy by the oversight of overbearing others. Both are simplistic, gross distortions. Holiness is neither.

As a teenager I couldn't see holiness clearly through the lens of my own somewhat narcissistic, ego-centered search for self. Such a search can last a lifetime. The social/behavioral expectations of family and church came into conflict with an expansive exercise of free will and attempts at personal independence. Life became more difficult and complex and compartmentalized. My head seemed to be in one place, my heart in another, and my will hunkered down in a stubborn funk.

Holiness for me became only an external way of life, mostly rules to follow, rules that demanded compliance. Then in later adolescence, with exposure to older and admired exemplars, my ideas of holiness changed. Holiness became defined more by spiritually inspiring, elite role models I was supposed to emulate. This I tried often without success. Fortunately, this would change in my college years.

The Bible makes it very clear. Holiness is the desire of God's heart for everyone. It's part of God's perfect, loving kindness and plan for our shalom, life's ultimate fulfillment. Being made holy is being fully restored to the life that God desires for everyone. It's not for a few, but for all. It's more than salvation from sin and guilt. God intends our complete freedom from the bondage and power of sin, a liberation to holiness in the likeness of Christ and purity of heart and life. Holiness is meant to prepare us for God's service.

Scripture also underscores that salvation from the penalty and guilt of sin and holiness are both free gifts of grace that we receive by faith. As such, the pursuit and experience of holiness increasingly opens the way to a deeper life of intimate love of God and amazing love for others. Far from being undesirable, it is the ultimate, desirable condition of the heart, enabling us to live a godly life, and by God's grace freed to love God and others with a pure heart.

Some people remain confused by thinking that holiness is unobtainable. They wrongly believe that holiness sets the bar too high. If it is the high road, it seems too steep and exhausting. It requires a spiritual stamina beyond one's capacity. The Bible is clear that God's desire is that all persons experience a full salvation *from* the guilt and penalty of sin and *to* having power over sin, growing in grace and Christlikeness, and being filled with the fullness of God. Those ideals seem to remain obtainable.

There also is much confusion because of the idea that holiness is restricted. Over the centuries the church has restricted the idea of sainthood to a formal action of the Pope of Rome. Sainthood is understood to be a certification of holiness bestowed by the highest office within an ecclesiastical structure. It's viewed by common people as an honor available only to a very few, when in truth saints are holy, humble, and common people. They are sinners redeemed, reconciled, and restored to the holy likeness of Christ.

Holiness is not an inaccessible idea when seen through an ecological lens. Saints, holy people, are grown. The process is organic.

God uses the fertile soil of the hearts of sanctified others in whose company the seed of an individual's life in the Spirit is entrusted. In this way, God produces in us the fruit of others' faithfulness and obedience (John 15:5). In short, we may call the company of saintly others God's garden patches where new life in Christ sprouts up, is nurtured into maturity, and fulfills God's intended plan of sanctification. All this is to the glory of the Creator/Gardener (John 15:1). God's garden patches and vineyards are the socially spiritual contexts (ecologies) of holiness.

Many people view holiness as optional. It's considered just another alternative lifestyle. In both the Old and New Testaments, however, God gives the directive, "Be holy." It's not a suggestion nor an option. It's God's expectation in the form of a command. Nevertheless, many Christians are satisfied to treat holiness as optional. John Wesley wrote about people who pursue salvation from sin but do not go on to holiness. In his sermon *The More Excellent Way*[6], he writes about high-road and low-road Christians. The high road is one of holiness. It's not optional for those who wish to see God. Scripture says, "Without holiness no one will see God" (Hebrews 12:14).

It's not surprising that few people pursue holiness when they think it's inaccessible, unavailable, merely optional, even undesirable. But if holiness is not any of these things, what is it?

What Holiness Is

To understand holiness, we must start by understanding the identity of the risen Christ. This is what happened to the two confused disciples on the road to Emmaus. In the company of Jesus they were exposed to the Messiah, the Lord and Master full of grace and truth (John 1:14). As he walked with them he opened the Scriptures to them. Why had he come, who was he really, and what did his life, death, and resurrection really mean? Their confusion dissipated.

Their worldview was deconstructed and then reconstructed. Their understanding of the Kingdom and God's purpose for their salvation was clarified. All this occurred in the presence of the resurrected Christ as he revealed himself finally in the breaking of the bread.

This journey with Christ was more than a social event and pleasant experience. Though Scripture does not say this explicitly, we may assume that these travelers to Emmaus took a turn toward a more excellent way of faith and a restoration of hope. In the social context of their Lord's presence, they were transformed and never again the same. The same socially spiritual presence and power of God in the hearts and lives of people is real today. It's found in interpersonal relationships and encounters with others and with God that lead to a more excellent way.

Not many years ago there lived George Allen Turner, a revered professor of New Testament at Asbury Theological Seminary. I came to know him in the last years of his life. In his book *The More Excellent Way,* he writes, "While the terms associated with 'holiness' stress the contrast between Jehovah and humanity, bridged by an act of cleansing, those associated with 'perfection' point to humanity's kinship with God and the possibility of fellowship."[7] That one sentence is pregnant with the idea of the social-relational, interpersonal nature of holiness.

The ideas of cleansing and perfection speak about a restorative work of God in a person's life. Cleansing suggests purity of heart and life, making possible a person's intimacy with God. Kinship with God suggests the hallowed, social setting of family and inclusion into an ongoing, close-knit, intimate relationship with the three persons of the Godhead. Finally, the possibility of fellowship with God implies an ongoing, interactive, interpersonal relationship in the context of acquaintance and intimacy with God.

Diane Leclerc puts it this way. "Only God is holy. Yet God commands, 'Be holy as I am holy.'"[8] She makes the case that humanity derives holiness from relationship with God and the quality of that relationship. Holiness involves imparted righteousness dependent through an ongoing social, relational connection with God. Such a relationship makes possible God's multiple acts of grace, including forgiveness of sin, reconciliation with God, initial sanctification, continuing (synergistic) sanctification, the progressive restoration to the likeness of Christ, and ultimately entire sanctification and purity of heart, all to the glory of God.

When we say sanctification, we also mean holiness. The words are interchangeable. Samuel Logan Brengle writes this in *The Way of Holiness*:

> Sanctification is to have our sinful tempers cleansed, and the heart filled with love to God and man.... The Bible teaches that we can be like Jesus. We are to be like him in our separation from the world, in purity, in love, and in the fullness of the Spirit. This is holiness... a clean heart in which the Holy Spirit dwells, filling it with pure, tender, and constant love to God and Man.... There is a plant in South America called the "pitcher plant" on the stalk of which, below each leaf, is a little cup-like formation that is always full of water. When it is very small it is full; as it grows larger it is still full; and when it reaches maturity it is full. That illustrates holiness. All that God asks is that the hearer should be cleansed from sin and full of love, whether it be the tender heart of the little child with feeble powers of loving, or of the full-grown man, or of the flaming archangel before the Throne.[9]

When filled with holy love in the context of continued obedience, the heart will grow more and more like Brengle's South American pitcher plant. It will then be filled even more and more with the holy love of God.

More recently, Roger Green has written, "Holiness is a life of obedience, rooted in love, to the Great Commandment of our Lord—to love God and our neighbor supremely.... Obedience is the natural outcome of that love for God, and so we are compelled to love our neighbor also."[10] Frederick Coutts writes that the experience of holiness may be "defined as one in which the whole person is redirected towards the highest spiritual end, likeness to Christ, and in this he is granted the continual help of the Holy Spirit."[11]

Notice in these clarifications of holiness the pattern of God's grace and our response. God fills and cleanses, we exercise obedient faith in love to God and others, and God redirects us toward the likeness of Jesus with the continual help of the Spirit. God is always the prime mover. The pattern is God's grace first and our obedient response in return. I am reminded of the chorus by John Gowans often sung in my faith community:

To be like Jesus!
This hope possesses me,
In every thought and deed,
This is my aim, my creed.
To be like Jesus!
This hope possesses me.
His Spirit helping me,
Like Him I'll be.

Moving into God's House

Kevin M. Watson likens sanctification to moving all of one's life into God's house. He says, "If repentance is the porch of God's house, and faith the door, the new birth is when you cross the threshold of God's house, and holiness is the process of moving our lives completely into God's house."[12] From the beginning of our salvation, being "born again," the moving in is a gradual work of sanctification.

To press the metaphor, by moving in, enabled by the Holy spirit, we get rid of all the junk, the trash accumulated over time by our dispositions, habits, and sins. The more we discard, the more we are dead to sin. We progress from grace to grace, being conformed to the likeness of Jesus, waiting for that encounter with God when we receive full salvation from all sin, our entire sanctification, or what John Wesley called our going on to perfection, perfect love. We don't do this on our own. Other saints come alongside and help us move in entirely and remain a resident.

Wesley cited the Apostle Paul's benediction, "Now may the God of peace Himself sanctify you completely; and may your whole spirit, soul, and body be preserved blameless at the coming of our Lord Jesus Christ. He who calls you is faithful, who also will do it" (1 Thessalonians 5:23-24, NKJV). Wesley went on to say:

> It is thus that we wait for entire sanctification; for a full salvation from all our sins, from pride, self-will, anger, unbelief; or, as the Apostle expresses it, "go on unto perfection." But what is perfection? The word has various senses: Here it means perfect love. It is love excluding sin; love filling the heart, taking up the whole capacity of the soul. It is love "rejoicing evermore, praying without ceasing, in everything giving thanks."[13]

Entire sanctification is God's cleansing that leaves a pure heart, makes possible inward holiness, outward righteousness, and continuing growth in grace. Holiness is reflected in a profound holy love of God and a profound love for others (Mark 12:30-31). It occasions an inner moral transformation that is expressed in holy love made possible not only to some, but to all.

Most simply defined, holiness is Christ-likeness, the unfolding of Jesus Christ's own character in the life of the believer who devotes time and attention to the way of holiness, that is, deliberately remaining in a sanctified context. That context is God's presence as the Holy Spirit working through the presence of holy others. It's the Spirit making possible spiritual growth, formation, Christ-likeness, and ultimately a cleansing of the heart, soul, and mind to the glory of God.

What about social holiness? Consistent with Kevin Watson's holiness move-in metaphor, the Holy Spirit guides us in repentance, helping to get us onto the porch, cross the threshold, and through the front door. Our status is not that of temporary guests, but real members of God's family. It's an occasion of social holiness in that the Holy Spirit uses others, human agency, in the process. God uses the company of others to guide, support, and encourage us to participate in the blessing of inclusive, sanctified family life. The Spirit uses the example and encouragement of others to immerse us in various means of grace that help us grow in the likeness of the home's owners: The Father, Son, and Holy Spirit.

Others help us unpack, find the kitchen and bedroom, and enjoy the fellowship of life among saints in the intimate presence of God. God provides others to coach us and help us understand the responsibilities and chores that need to be done, especially in helping others find the porch, move in, and become intimate members of God's family.[14]

All metaphors have shortfalls. Kevin Watson's move-in metaphor for holiness may be too static, just sitting in a house. A journey metaphor, walking daily with Christ in the Spirit, moving on with God in mission, may complement and balance Watson's more static image of the process of gaining holiness.

Holiness is social in that it is the desire of the Trinity for us whose nature is intimately social. It is God's desire to include us in the holiness project and reach out to others to bring them to the table of holy fellowship, and invite them to the divine dance. In Wesley's words, we are called to "spread Scriptural holiness across the land." Social holiness is the desire of God the Father and the continuing work of Jesus the Son by the agency of the Holy Spirit. God gets the sanctifying work done in part through the participation and influence of sanctified others who are means of God's sanctifying grace.

It's the privilege of all believers in Christ to be wholly sanctified, to participate in the divine nature (2 Peter 1:4), and to reflect the image of Christ to the world. By the Holy Spirit and the faithfulness of others, God is restoring all of humanity to that image, the *Imago Dei*. Social holiness is at the heart of God's new creation project. It's central in God's desire to save all people from the uttermost of sin to the uttermost of holiness and intimacy with Him.

God could do all of this without human assistance, but chooses to do it for us and then through us by the agency of holy others. Holiness is social in that it comes to us from God in part through others and then is passed on to others by God's work in and through us.

DISCUSSION QUESTIONS

1. Of all the ways to think about holiness, what ways to you find most helpful?

2. Does Brengle's example of holiness being like a pitcher plant make sense to you?

3. Would you say that your idea of holiness is clear or foggy?

4. Do others play a role in your obedience to God's directive, "Be holy!" In what ways?

5. If holiness is Christ-likeness, who is helping you pursue Christ-likeness?

6. If sanctification is like moving into God's house, where are you in the moving process?

three

STOPS ALONG THE WAY

Not that I have already obtained all this,
or have already been made perfect,
but I press on to take hold of that
for which Christ took hold of me.

Philippians 3:12

Throughout life we enjoy and sometimes suffer the company of thousands of others, some friends and some acquaintances, some very impactful and others not so much. The impactful ones influence us particularly when we are one-on-one or together in small groups.

In reflection, how often have you been one-on-one with a friend? You knew him or her well only to learn something new, something different, something more. You were more than well acquainted. You were close friends. Then the person shared something new, something deep and unexpected, something transformational. What was said made you think. It made an impression on your heart and opened a new possibility, a new way of looking at life, a new pathway to pursue.

Not long ago my daughter met a young man at church. He seemed nice, friendly, and polite, but that's all. They had a mutual friend they liked and respected. One day the mutual friend asked the young man if he had ever thought about asking my daughter for a date. He thought about it and eventually did ask her to play a round of tennis. That was the beginning.

Actually, that round of tennis was a life-changing turning point. Now, years later in their journey together, they are approaching their sixth wedding anniversary. Today I have a beloved son-in-law and two beautiful grandsons. It turned out that the young man has a hunger and thirst for God. Unlike many Christians, he is more than merely a Christ admirer. He is a serious follower, an answer to our prayers as parents of our wonderful daughter. Today we remain grateful to that mutual friend who brokered a first date.

This is how God's grace works in response to prayer. Through the company we keep, others bring God's grace into our daily lives. God's grace becomes transformational. Like the two disciples on the road to Emmaus, our journey takes turns for the best with the help of others.

A Road Trip with Jesus

Imagine yourself as one of the two disciples on that first, post-resurrection Sunday morning. Put yourself in the story (Luke 24:13-35). You're on your way from Jerusalem to Emmaus with a friend. You both were disciples who had followed Christ for three years. Now your following is over. You are walking to Emmaus and talking about the events of the last few days: the arrest of Jesus, the trial, the crucifixion, burial, and now the empty tomb. As you walk, you're both sad and confused. How is it possible? Jesus, the Messiah, is dead. You had been expecting the mind-blowing, life-changing event of Christ's coronation. Instead he was crucified, dead, and buried.

What you had hoped for just didn't happen, but what you don't realize that everything is about to change. Your eyes are going to be opened like the man blinded from birth that Jesus healed (John 9:1-7). Your preconceived notions about the Messiah are about to be washed away like the mud from the blind beggar's eyes. You're soon about to see all of life in a completely different light. Are you ready?

By the end of the day you make a remarkable discovery. Your journey is interrupted by someone you don't recognize. He comes alongside, a new social context. Beginning with Moses and the prophets, he explains what was said in the Scriptures concerning Jesus. In the company of the stranger, your worldview and way of life is forever altered, reconstructed, transformed. The unknown friend totally renovates your mind, your heart, your perspective, your worldview, your understanding of the Kingdom and Christ's work and love for you as your Messiah.

Then, leisurely over dinner, this friend breaks bread and prays. You have a flashback. You see that all along it is him, Christ Jesus! Exposures become encounter. Along the way, looking back, you realize that you now are encountering the Master, and in a deeper, more intimate, and possibly in a more disturbing way than ever before. You realize you will never be the same, that you will be forever in his company by the gift of the Holy Spirit (Acts 2:1-4).

Each of us differs in our walk with Jesus. As we progress in our faith journey, we each have our own Emmaus road. We find ourselves in the company of Jesus and others at different places and paces along the way. Some of us have journeyed enough to know Jesus somewhat, and then we stop. We settle into a partial view of the Kingdom of God. Our idea of salvation is limited and restricted to only being saved from past sin. Our Christian worldview is minimal and anemic, lacking in power and promise.

Others continue journeying down their faith roads and are privileged to come to know Jesus differently, deeply. Salvation becomes expansive and hopeful. God's grace is always new, fresh, open to discovery and occasions optimism for the future. Along the way, the company we keep on our journey becomes a guidepost and a GPS keeping us moving in the right direction while we walk increasingly in holiness and intimacy with Christ.

Every journey has its stops, but not everyone continues on to reach the intended destination. Some people wander without a destination. For whatever reasons, some stop after traveling only so far. They think they have finished the race when they've only reached the starting line.

For example, the history of the settlement of the American West includes the stories of many pioneers setting out for Oregon. Along the way some of them decided to go only part way and settle down. Some went as far as Missouri or Kansas and settled there. Some ventured on to Colorado and Arizona, while others, determined to reach Oregon, went as far as they had hoped. That's the story of many Christians in their faith journey, many stopping part way, some reaching the full destination.

No Bus-Stop Religion

So many Christians stop part way. They stop to admire Christ, not follow him. This is bus-stop religion. Salvation is often preached and taught only as a simple matter of forgiveness of sin. As a result, many get saved from sin and wait for the glory bus to take them to heaven. It's a simple religion that you won't find in the Bible, "get saved; go to heaven."

The idea is faulty if it's only repent of past sin and accept Christ as Savior, and that's it. That's all there is. For some believers, salvation is viewed as an individual achievement. We get busy reading the Bible now and then, helping out in the church, being kind to others, and just waiting the remainder of life for the glory bus to take us to heaven. It's like stopping in Kansas when the destination is Oregon.

Bus-stop religion is halfway salvation, salvation from sin that stops short of the whole gospel narrative. Instead of "full salvation," it's only half. The Bread of life, Jesus, is a full loaf, but people are taught to be satisfied with only a slice or two. The gospel proclaims not only salvation from sin, but also moving on to Christ-likeness and holy intimacy with God and holy self-giving to others.

That's what we mean by "full salvation." We're not meant to get saved and then stop. Our destination is not meant to be merely heaven one day. The Bible says, "Without holiness one will not see God" (Hebrews 12:14). The journey is toward a destination of holiness reflected in a profound love for God and a profound love for others (Mark 12:30-31), evidenced clearly in how we think and the way we live.

The Barna Study

George Barna has something to say about finishing the faith journey. Perhaps you've heard of the Barna Group, a research firm specializing in the study of religious beliefs and the spiritual behavior of Americans. One particular study captures the road trip of faith in all its stops.[15]

The Barna findings in question underscore the truth that wherever we are on our journey, *we should not stop.* There is always more: more ground to gain, more heights to discover, greater vistas to enjoy, more grace from God. Barna and his colleagues discovered this by studying a spectrum of the American population and people's faith development.

Over a six-year period, fifteen thousand people were surveyed in search of their pitfalls and challenges in faith development. All of those surveyed were American citizens, a random sample not limited to Christians. The focus of the study was how Americans assessed their own faith development and progress. The results were unexpected and astounding. Barna and company found that people self-assess themselves by one of "ten transformational stops" or categories seen in percentages as follows:

TEN TRANSFORMATIONAL STOPS

1. Unaware of Sin — 1%
2. Indifferent to Sin — 16%
3. Worried About Sin — 39%
4. Forgiven for Sin — 9%
5. Busy in Church Activities — 24%
6. Holy Discontent — 6%
7. Broken by God — 3%
8. Surrender & Submission — 1%
9. Profound Love of God — 0.5%
10. Profound Love of People — 0.5%

These results are an eye opener. They bring to light where the American public stands on the issue of faith and spiritual development. The great majority of survey responders are found in categories three to five. Eighty-nine percent of the responders, representative of the U.S. population, are found in the first five categories. At the same time, only eleven percent fall between the six and ten stops. Barna calls these "stops" because it is at these ten points that various groups appear to stop in their faith development and transformation.

In the light of Bus-Stop Religion (my metaphor), one percent of Americans are unaware of sin and don't know there is a bus. Sixteen percent don't care. They are indifferent to sin. Of the fifteen thousand responders to the survey, thirty-nine percent are worried about sin and whether they should catch the bus.

A total of fifty-six percent of people in the survey never get on the bus. They never seek a salvation of justifying grace. Another nine percent seek forgiveness for sin and get on the bus, but their bus is permanently parked at the church, with another twenty-four percent going on to engage in church activities to keep them busy doing good.

Overall, as seen in this Barna study data, eighty-nine percent of the population stop at one of five bus stops somewhere along the way and progress at best half way. Only eleven percent of the population goes on to stops six through ten. Out of the eighty-nine percent of the population at the first five stops, J. D. Walt describes it something like this. You're a sinner. You need a Savior. Pray this prayer and you're good to go. Now get busy in the activities of the church.[16]

DISCUSSION QUESTIONS

1. When was the last time someone came alongside of you and helped you to see things more clearly?

2. Do you know anyone stuck at Barna's stop #2 or has returned back to #2?

3. Where do you place yourself along Barna's ten transformational stops?

4. Where would you like to be?

four

THE JOURNEY OF MAXIMUM FAITH

Let us keep in step with the Spirit.

Galatians 5:25

I n his book *Maximum Faith*, George Barna gives the background of his study that we highlighted in chapter three. He lays out the ten transformational stops as the path to people's maximum faith and wholeness. More than a description of the stops and sequence along the way, he describes the journey as one of maximum faith and wholeness. Sadly, so few exercise maximum faith and continue the journey. For a variety of reasons, the overwhelming majority of persons (89%) fail to progress through the stops.

Barna is not suggesting that the journey is always by a straight path sequentially through each stop. But he does suggest there are five possible paths, four of which he characterizes as "mindless mutiny" or "hopeless meandering" leading to stops on the path. He discusses five paths:

THE TEN TRANSITIONAL STOPS

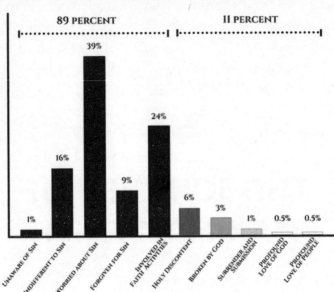

1. Moving sequentially from one to ten.

2. Settling for religiosity, stopping at #6, holy discontent, but in reality settling for #5, involved in faith activities.

3. Exploiting cheap grace, getting to #6, holy discontent, but reverting back to #2, indifference to sin.

4. Becoming angry with God, progressing through #6, holy discontent, but when getting to #7, broken by God, becoming angry with God who would subject anyone to such a process of testing. They often return as well to #2, indifference to sin.

5. Traveling the biblical path and leaping from #3, worried about sin, to #7, broken by God and continuing onwards.

Barna's study suggests that humanity's great struggle spiritually is ignorance, disobedience, and/or indifference to sin. It's no wonder that most people stop halfway on the journey. Unlike the Apostle Paul, they don't "press on to take hold of that for which Christ took hold of them" (Philippians 3:12). They discontinue the roadtrip with Jesus. They become satisfied with stops far short of God's intended best. They settle into a comfort zone of complacency, taking themselves out of the soul-shaping hands of God.

Sadly, even in the context of church life, so many believers remain blind, deaf, and/or dumb to the reality that there is more, always more. Some appreciate the possibilities of more, but are unwilling to respond to the Spirit who counsels and encourages continuing the journey.

Why would anyone stop? We may look for answers in the social/spiritual milieu that leaves them in the dark about a more excellent way. They remain high and dry rather than immersed in the fullness of God, baptized by the Holy Spirit.

Plowing Up a Snake

When the religious leaders, Sadducees and Pharisees, got together in discourse with Jesus, one of them, an expert in the law, asked him, "Teacher, which is the greatest commandment in the Law?" Jesus replied, "Love the Lord your God with all your heart and with all your soul and with all your mind." This is the first and greatest commandment. And the second is like it: "Love your neighbor as yourself. All the Law and the Prophets hang on these two commandments" (Matthew 22:36-40).

In the Barna study, the two maximum transformational stops, numbers nine and ten, are profound the love of God and the profound love of others. If becoming people who love God and others profoundly is the aim of the spiritual life, what's wrong with the picture of today's church? What's missing that can help to sustain a person's journey of maximum faith?

There is an old expression that my friend Jerry Michael used to repeat. When a topic was raised that made people uncomfortable and no one wanted to deal with it, he would say, "Someone just plowed up a snake." George Barna's study has plowed up a proverbial snake, and J. D. Walt recognizes it for what it is.

In two essays on the Barna study, Walt raises two concerns that hit the very center of the matter. Walt's first essay is "What Happened to the Whole Gospel: Getting On with the Second Half of Salvation?"[17] The second essay gets at the problem behind the first concern. It's titled "The Problem with Growing Churches."[18]

In the first essay, Walt asks, "How can we have so much religious activity in a nation and so little to show for it? People are going halfway with the Lord, but not the rest of the way. The study reveals a faith that is high on faith decisions and low on discipleship; high on justification and low on sanctification." Precisely. The majority of Americans who claim to be Christians need to move on from just being busy in the church to a profound love of God and others. Along the way, there is no skipping over holy discontent, being broken by God, surrendering, and submission.

The whole world is stuck in sin while the church is stuck in the inward activity of being church, a position of stasis, static activity, possibly better described as slumber, in deep sleep with no forward movement. The great commandment of Jesus calls the Body of Christ to wake up and get going. What's missing is dynamic movement in the direction of holiness. The Body needs to move beyond justification to sanctification, to a full salvation to the praise of God's glory and the good of all people.

What's the problem? It's falling short. It's settling for less when there's more. If God's commandment is truly great, what's stopping the church from responding in obedience? The Barna study highlights the big problem of shortfall. The title of J. D. Walt's second essay plows up another snake by suggesting the problem behind the problem, the church.

In his second article, "The Problem with Growing Churches," Walt juxtaposes two problems of the church in North America today. The first is that the church is not growing. The second is that people in the church are not growing, not moving forward beyond stops four and five. Even in the churches that are growing, are they growing their people? Not really. Whether churches are growing or not in numbers, they are not growing people. People's spiritual growth is prematurely arrested, stuck in the early stages of spiritual development.

Walt suggests the reason for this is that church leaders are asking how to grow churches in size, how to get more people in the door, how to engage them in more church activity and programs.[19] The problem? "Aren't these the wrong questions? Shouldn't the questions needing to be asked be, 'Who do you want your people to become?'" More importantly, "Who do *you* want to become?" What are the necessary conditions and contexts for the needed growth?

These are questions of sanctifying aspiration. Other related questions are these. What does the heart, mind, and soul look like when someone has a profound love of God and others? Who are they who respond to holy discontent and brokenness, to submission and surrender, and who go to profound depths in their love of God and others? How do they become a people transformed into the image of God, filled to the measure of the fullness of God? (Ephesians 3:2, 19).

My own denomination is struggling with this problem. A former international leader of The Salvation Army, John Gowans, once declared, "The Salvation Army was 'invented' to save souls, grow saints, and serve suffering humanity."[20] This is a strong statement capturing the essence of The Salvation Army's mission. It also aligns itself with the theology of John Wesley and his *via salutis*. Salvation is more than a journey to being saved from sin, Barna's stop number five. It's also the journey of being entirely sanctified, moving on to stops nine and ten, holiness and righteous.

Saving souls is a mission of meeting the human needs of others with the prospect of full salvation, all the stops being accounted for. It includes the process of maturing saints who grow in grace to become believers formed in the likeness of Christ, filled with the Spirit, loving and serving others to the glory of God. To truly save souls, grow saints, and love and serve suffering others, one must want to become *fully saved*, continually growing as a saint and faithfully loving and therefore sacrificially serving others.

J. D. Walt has put his finger on the pulse of many churches and their leaders in the Wesleyan Holiness tradition. While working hard at growing the church, one's own pulse is weak. The pulse of the faith community and denomination is weak because the heart is yearning to grow the church in size more than to grow people, including themselves, to be participants of the divine nature. The focus must be on what the church and the ministry can become in Christ and for Christ. Then, when people become filled to the measure of the fullness of God, God can do immeasurably more in them, through them, and among them for the Kingdom of God. There's nothing wrong with that picture!

Now, does this have anything to do with social holiness and the company we keep? This is a difficult question for many Christians who have a foggy idea of a full salvation, especially of Barna's stops six through ten. They lack clarity about what holiness is and isn't. Their ideas about holiness are mistaken, misguided, and erroneous. Their thinking about holiness is dysfunctional and occasions an arrested spiritual development. They desperately need to gain clarity and then actually "press on."

In the words of the Apostle Paul, "Not that I have already obtained all this, or have already arrived at my goal, but I press on to take hold of that for which Christ Jesus took hold of me. I do not consider myself yet to have taken hold of it. But one thing I do:

Forgetting what is behind and straining toward what is ahead, I press on toward the goal to win the prize for which God has called me heavenward in Christ Jesus" (Philippians 3:2,17).

DISCUSSION QUESTIONS

1. What do you think about your church? Does it have a problem with growing?

2. What problem is it working on, growing in size, spiritually maturing its members, or both?

3. Proverbs 13:20 says, "He who walks with the wise grows wise, but a companion of fools suffers harm." First Corinthians 15:33 says, "Bad company corrupts character." With whom are you walking and keeping company?

4. Is your church helping you progress toward maximum faith? If so, how?

five

IN THE ZONE

*"For as a belt is bound around a man's waist,
so I bound the whole house of Israel and the whole
house of Judah to me," declares the Lord, "to be
my people for my renown, and praise, and honor."*

Jeremiah 13:11

Social holiness is all about being "in the zone," in close proximity to and in frequent, sustained, and interpersonal contact with God. This often is with the help of others. In the Book of Jeremiah (13:1-22) we read a story about the importance of remaining in the zone, in the sphere of influence. It reminds us of something Jesus said to his disciples when he shared with them the Last Supper. He directed them to remain in him if they were to bear fruit (John 15:5).

In Jeremiah's story God likens the people of Israel and Judah to the linen belt that God directed Jeremiah to wear around his waist. The belt was not to touch water. Jeremiah obeyed, put it around his waist, and wore it. Then God told him to take off the belt and put it down in the crevice of a rock, submerging it in the damp bank of the river. Though that may have seemed strange, Jeremiah obeyed. Later God told him to retrieve the belt and he did. When Jeremiah found the belt, it was "ruined and completely useless." Over time, in the wrong place, under the wrong conditions, it had rotted.

Like Jeremiah's belt, God's people put themselves in the wrong place for a long time. They turned away, distanced themselves from God, and fell into idolatry. Like the belt, they were ruined. God had bound them to himself. They were to cling to him. Intimacy as a people with God was to be their first priority. The core principle was to keep their hearts in proximity to God's heart, but they distanced themselves from God and pursued other gods. By their disobedience, they failed to stay in the most important zone, the company of God. Instead, as a people they chose the toxic company of pseudo-gods.

When we say "in the zone" in relation to holiness, we mean in the presence of God, near to the divine heart, and in the company of persons who themselves are intimate with God. The influence of God through others is thereby powerful and effective. God shapes the character and faith of those who keep God's company and through whom God goes on to transform the lives of others.

The opposite is sadly true. Disaster arises in the toxic company of those who live in divine disobedience. Eve was in the zone of Satan and fell prey to the snake in the garden. She persuaded Adam to be in the wrong zone as well (Genesis 3:1-7). Fast forwarding, Abram and his nephew Lot were looking over the pastures to graze the abundance of sheep God had provided. Although Abram was Lot's elder and mentor, he was willing to give his nephew the greener pastures near the towns of Sodom and Gomorrah. Abram moved his extended family, servants, and cattle to less desirable yet spiritually healthier environs. Lot and his household moved into a spiritually dangerous zone. There they were exposed to the prolonged influence of two morally toxic towns that today are metaphors for sin and degradation (Genesis 13:12-13).

Scripture is full examples of saints whose faithful walk with God established a zone of divine influence and character. God used Moses as a mentor to shape Joshua into his successor who would lead Israel into the promised land. Joshua spent forty years in the Moses zone (Deuteronomy 31:14, 23). Gideon was the youngest son of a poor farmer in a country that had no army, government, or any infrastructure and was continually besieged by enemies. God brought Gideon into the zone of the divine presence and blessed him through a sequence of challenges. Gideon's success was contingent on his continued proximity to God and obedient faith. Ultimately, the result was complete victory over Israel's enemies followed by forty years of peace (Judges 8:28). Sadly, in the end, Gideon distanced himself from God. His obedient faith dissipated and he fell into idolatry (Judges 8:27).

David was in the zone of the Holy Spirit when Samuel anointed him as a young boy to be Israel's future king. At that moment "the Spirit of the Lord came upon David in power" (1 Samuel 16:13). He became by far Israel's greatest king. Over his three years of ministry, Jesus was a teacher of thousands, but he was especially a mentor to those who were in his immediate sphere of influence as disciples, including the two that day on the road to Emmaus (Luke 24:13-35). Timothy came into the zone of Paul's influence when Paul mentored him as a junior partner in his ministry (1 Timothy 4:1-15).

Scripture is filled with stories of God's grace shared through the influence and persuasion of mentors who came alongside and gave wisdom and counsel to others. Proverbs 15:22 says, "Plans fail for the lack of counsel, but with many advisors they succeed." There are recorded encounters of obedient saints who lived directly in the zone of God's presence and power and by the Holy Spirit channeled God's grace to others. Sometimes God chooses to act alone, but more often uses others. Regardless, the grace is always God's.

Alternative Zones of Benign Neglect

Until age twenty-one I lived in family, church, and Christian college zones of guidance and preparation for a blessed life of holiness unto the Lord. Then things changed. In my five years of doctoral studies in a public university, I discovered that even a strong faith can dissipate. It happens when consecration drifts to commitment, and commitment slips into casual, only occasional interest in God. Then dissipation of faith occasions a reversal of growth in grace. We may not lose our salvation, but at least we drift out of good relationship and face significant consequences.

John Wesley wrote a sermon on the matter of dissipation in which he said, "We are accustomed to speak of dissipation as having respect chiefly, if not wholly, to the outward behaviour, to the manner of life. But it takes place within before it appears without. It is in the heart before it is seen in outward conversation. There must be a dissipated spirit before there is a dissipated manner of life."[21] His text for this sermon was 1 Corinthians 7:35 (NKJV), "This I speak that ye may attend upon the Lord without distraction."

The Apostle Paul uses the word distraction in another translation (TNIV): "I am saying this for your own good, not to restrict you, but that you may live in the right way in undivided devotion to the Lord." The context for Paul's comment is the situation that challenges us all. We become too "concerned about the affairs of this world" (1 Corinthians 7:34). We become distracted from undivided devotion to God. We drift into a divided heart and begin exercising benign neglect of our relationship with God. This is so subtle and easy to do.

We live in a time of enormous distractions: sports, cable TV, video games, online buying, Facebook, politics, tweeting, texting, and more. Distractions, however good and legitimate, steal our time, divert our attention, and erode our capacity for devotion. Time and attention go to things other than keeping company with

God. Devotion is diverted to countless lesser pursuits. Christ takes a second, third, or fourth place in our priorities. While God is present and does not abandon us, nevertheless we stop paying attention and drift in our faith.

This was my situation for the five years I was working on my doctoral degree. It was not that I plunged into terrible sins and shameful behaviors. It was more a matter of putting God on hold, practicing benign neglect. Faith became dormant and static. Other priorities emerged and worked to divide my heart. With distractions and diversions came a dissipation of my faith. The well became nearly dry. The fire was down to a mere ember. The bread for the journey became mere crumbs. The process of soul care slowly diminished. I had taken the clay of my life off the Potter's wheel.

This was my situation. In my journey with God, I had stepped off the bus. I had drifted into a new and different zone during five years of doctoral studies. For the first time in my life I was immersed in a secular, social/intellectual milieu called graduate school. I was a relatively mature Christian with a passion for holiness, but the context was distracting in large part because it was demanding. To get through the doctoral ordeal, I had become an intellectual workaholic. I became subtly and imperceptibly detached from that to which I had been so devoted. I wasn't aware that in the process of dissipation I became unhitched, untethered to Christ, out of his zone of influence.

By the end of those fateful five years I had become a nominal Christian. Instead of a hunger and thirst for time with God in holiness and righteousness, I emerged with a doctoral degree and a tepid, divided heart. The flame of holy living, previously fanned by the Spirit and the many agents of God who were my sphere of influence, was nearly extinguished. Nevertheless, God was always present. Though faith may dissipate, God is faithful and patient, a God of restoration. God provided for me a means of grace to restore my faith and help me move from a spiritually barren zone of secular intellectualism back into the company of friends, mentors, and exemplars whose influences by God's grace were instrumentally salvific.

In the Zone of Mentors and Exemplars

Zones of social holiness are established when obedient, faithful teachers, mentors, and exemplars exert significant influence on others. Beyond their areas of expertise, mentors and exemplars are often admired and looked up to for their integrity and virtue. They are appreciated for their experience, wisdom, values, and character. Their influence often exceeds their intentions. For instance, John Wesley influenced major protagonists of his day in the fight against slavery. This was the case with William Wilberforce.

William Wilberforce (1759-1833) came into the zone and influence of John Wesley (1703-1791), his mentor in Wesley's later years. There was a difference of fifty-six years in their ages. Wilberforce was an English politician and philanthropist. He had come to faith in Christ under Wesley's preaching and grew in his faith in the context of their friendship. Wilberforce was a member of Parliament and a major player in the fight against slavery in Britain and America. In Wesley's last letter to Wilberforce, he wrote to underscore his concerns and opposition to slavery and to encourage Wilberforce to take action for change. He wrote:

Dear Sir:

Unless God has raised you up for this very thing, you will be worn out by the opposition of men and devils. But if God be for you, who can be against you? Are all of them together stronger than God? O, Be not weary of well doing! Go on in the name of God and the power of his might, till even American slavery (the vilest that ever saw the sun) shall vanish away before it.... That he who has guided you from youth up may continue to strengthen you in all things, is the prayer of, dear sir,

Your affectionate servant,
John Wesley[22]

Wesley was passionately opposed to slavery and shared his lifelong passion in this last letter, encouraging young Wilberforce to go on in the fight that lasted for the next forty-two years. At the very end of Wesley's life he read the biography of Gustavas Vassa, a man born in Africa, kidnapped and sold into slavery. The book made a strong impression on Wesley, so much so that Wilberforce recorded his last words. It read, "John Wesley, his last words, Slave trade." Those words echoed in the heart of Wilberforce who subsequently wrote, "In the same spirit in which the old crusader put off his armor, the young crusader girded his on."

A few days before the 1791 Abolition debate in Parliament, Wilberforce wrote, "May I look to Him for wisdom and strength and the power of persuasion. And ascribe to Him all praise if I succeed." The fight was successful when the British parliament finally passed the Slavery Abolition Act in 1833. William Wilberforce died later that year. In obedience, Wesley lived in the zone of God's presence and inspired Wilberforce to live there as well. It was social holiness in action, as clear an example as I've ever encountered.

The company we keep can be powerful when we pursue a dynamic, synergistic partnership with God and others. While the guidance and friendship of Wesley with Wilberforce lasted only a brief number of years, the young Wilberforce was affected by Wesley for the remainder of his life and persisted in the mission Wesley had passed on to him. Wesley and God became the company Wilberforce kept.

Another Kind of Company

The company we keep can be alive and physically present, but also occasioned by someone whose thoughts we only read. The writings of others can put us in the zone of their influence. While sermons and lectures have an impact, the impact is perishable. Often much of what is shared is forgotten by the time the benediction is completed. The spoken word is perishable. The written word is less so.

Martin Luther King, Jr. (1929-1968) was a divinity student at Boston University in the 1950s. At that time he began reading E. Stanley Jones' writings (*Christ of the Indian Road, Christ of the American Road, The Word Become Flesh*, etc.) that he found in the school's library. Jones (1884-1973) was a missionary to India throughout much of the twentieth century. He always wrote about Christ being at the center of his missionary ministry in India for fifty-five years. Jones also wrote extensively about his long-time friend, Mahatma Gandhi (1869-1944). Through his writings, Jones introduced King to Gandhi. The intimacy of that friendship had a lasting and highly significant impact on Martin Luther King.

While Jones lived in the zone of Christ, Gandhi and King were in the zone of Jones. He was the literary company King kept. As a result, King came to know, appreciate, and emulate the non-violent, political strategies of Gandhi whom he had never actually met. Reflecting on John Wesley, William Wilberforce, E. Stanley Jones, Mahatma Gandhi, and Martin Luther King, Jr., we see that holiness and righteousness come to us through others and are passed on, sometimes impacting countless millions of others with their offspring, social justice. This is social holiness at its best.

In the Zone of Faithfulness

We also see the impact of social holiness and common grace on the life of Nelson Mandela. Grace, forgiveness, kindness, generosity of spirit, love for all, and redemption are just a few words I heard used to describe someone on a Sunday morning TV program that usually deals with politics. The spiritual tone of the discussion and the high and lofty attributions made me think I was in church. It sounded like a religious program, but the commentators weren't talking about Jesus. The focus was on Nelson Mandela. I found myself agreeing with much of the lofty, laudatory rhetoric. God placed him on the world stage and used him in an amazing way.

I continued to reflect on the program's discussion. As it was aired just after his death, I wondered if Mandela had a personal history that would explain the exceedingly kind words used on the program by luminaries like poet Maya Angelou, Harvard University Law School professor Charles Ogletree, and others. I began to ask myself if Mandela had a relationship with Jesus. For several years, I returned to that question. The answer in part may be found in the influence of the Methodist school system in South Africa.

By his own testimony, Methodists were central to Nelson Mandela's education throughout his early life, even during law school. In his movement through the Methodist school system, he remained in "the Methodist zone" of faithfulness. This is evident in his autobiography, *Long Walk to Freedom*.[23] Throughout the book he mentions the Methodist schools he attended and their influence on him from first grade through college. They included the Methodist mission school attached to the Thembu palace while he lived with his guardians following the death of his father. There his guardian, Chief Jongintaba Dalindyebo, took Mandela to church every Sunday. At age sixteen, he attended the Methodist Clarkebury College for two years, receiving an associates degree. Then he attended the Healdton Comprehensive School of the Methodists for two more years, followed by the Methodist University at Fort Hare, where he completed his bachelors degree in 1943.

According to his autobiography, until his entry into law school at the University of Whitwatersland, all of Nelson Mandela's education took place within the Methodist educational system in South Africa. Even in law school Mandela roomed in the Wesley House dormitory. During that time in Methodist missions, there was still a strong emphasis on faith in Christ, growing in grace, and personal and social holiness. The Bible was integrated into the Methodist curriculum as an integral part of each student's education. For approximately two decades, Mandela was immersed in the social-spiritual milieu of Methodist education and residential life. It is likely that he even participated in Methodist class meetings that then were ubiquitous in Methodist community life.

All of this is mentioned in Mandela's autobiography, but we don't know much about his faith in Christ. We do know that in high school he taught a Bible study class to other students. We can imagine that the spiritual environment of his early years gave him much to ponder during the twenty-seven years that he spent in prison. This would answer the question of where Mandela's strength to forgive came from, where he acquired his enormous capacity for patience, his insistence on the dignity of all persons, and his kindness and personal warmth to his prison guards. This would explain the power of his spirit and its impact on all those with whom he came in contact. His prison life was transformational.

The two decades of faithful Christian education likely had much to do with the presence of God in Nelson Mandela's life. The zones of two socially transformative contexts were (1) Methodist educational settings for twenty years and (2) twenty-seven years in prison pondering earlier lessons learned. It's likely that his Methodist education informed his years of reflection and resulted in stunning the world with his post-incarceration policy of grace. Glory to God! Though now he has passed on to another life, he remains an exemplary figure in contemporary history for many who remember his life and influence well beyond the borders of South Africa.

My own belief is that Mandela's life was in the zone of the Holy Spirit working in and through him to bless the world. Just when the world looks scary or bleak, we see God's grace at work. "The wind blows wherever it pleases. You hear its sound, but you cannot tell where it comes from or where it is going" (John 3:8). Sometimes it's common grace as in Gandhi and sometimes it's reconciling grace, as in the life of Mandella. As all truth is God's truth, all grace is God's grace.

Social Holiness in Context

Social holiness is powerful. The company we keep is key to the kind of life we live. It informs what impact we may have on the world. As social holiness comes to us through others and is passed on, attitudes, values, perceptions of right and wrong, moral dispositions, and preferences are formed, and history unfolds ultimately to the glory of God.

The company of others influences the food we eat, the teams we champion, the fashions we follow, the music we listen to, and the priorities that determine how we spend our time and with whom. These areas in our lives are the foci of social psychology and also the foci of the relational theology of John Wesley. He wrote extensively about health, food, and diet, and what he called our tempers (dispositions).

Our tempers determine the nature of our spiritual beliefs and practices, the quality of our lives, the condition of our hearts, and our moral judgments, behaviors, and influence on others. They are formed by the company of others, the social/spiritual zones in which we spend our waking hours. Ultimately, social holiness is all about remaining in the zone, God's presence, the Holy Spirit's zone where we are empowered in love and equipped for influence and service.

Being in the zone means more than merely being in the company of another. While it can mean that, its use is often much broader. "In the zone" means in context, in the setting, in the dynamic, interactive, and synergistic presence of God and others. It entails being tuned into what others are doing, saying, aspiring to achieve, and their priorities, habits, and goals. It shapes our commitments. It covers the forces and sources of what influences our decisions and commitments. It means noticing realities about the lives of others and taking note of how those realities have meaning and importance for our own lives.

This is what often happens when young people, at the peak of their idealism, attend a Christian college or university contemplating what to do with life. They find themselves in a zone of formative influence. That's my story. Upon sitting in a psychology class taught by a gifted professor, I was fascinated by social psychology and dazzled by the professor. I tuned into not only the course content and its relevant applications to all of life around me. I also focused on the person of the teacher, who he was, his personable temper, kindness, and strength of character. He created a zone of holiness. He wasn't perfect, but it was obvious that he was being perfected in his pursuit of holiness of heart and life. That brought about a desire in me for a similar pursuit.

The more I observed this professor the more I aspired to be like him. I was in the zone of a mentor and exemplar. I took more courses from him, including directed readings. I worked really hard to earn good grades. Looking back, I was not so much in his zone as in the Spirit's zone that radiated from his life and that of his wife and family. They were God's special means of grace at that time in my life. It is not surprising that, through these exposures to Christ in them, God called me to be a professor like him. I went on to pursue doctoral studies in social psychology.

That's how God works. Social holiness is powerful when we are in the zone, in the right context, in the social/spiritual ecology of the Holy Spirit.

A God of Restoration

Earlier I shared about my dissipated faith when I went off to graduate school. Though my faith dissipated over my years of doctoral studies, nevertheless God was faithful. My earlier professor and his wife continued to be a zone of influence that carried me through those years and kept the embers of my soul alive. Unfortunately, at the time, God's grace in my life went unrecognized and unacknowledged because of the distractions. God restored my faith and helped me get back in step with Him. I was once again in the zone of God.

Over those five years, the fire in my soul and passion for God nearly went out. Still, God provided a way, a zone of influence of others that kept alive the flame of love for God. For several summers, my wife Irene and I worked at a Christian summer camp, one of The Salvation Army's sixty camp settings in North America. The camp was an ecology of human development and spiritual formation. My job was to run the camp's programs. This meant being the social, spiritual leader of the camp. The demands of the job required me to be in the Word, leading staff times of devotions, preaching children's sermons on Sundays, and spiritually counseling staff members through their own faith struggles.

I had to rise to the occasion each summer. In short, I was pumped up in my faith over two months each year in a redemptive, restorative, social/spiritual environment. I was restored within a sanctified social ecology, the small intentional community of a Christian summer camp. In those summer months I entered a zone of expectation that I would be a personal means of grace to all others in the camp community. The irony is that in the company of the camp staff, I found myself in the zone of a God of restoration.

Each summer I was in the zone where the staff's responses were God's means of grace for me. I had never left the zone of God's presence and love. The challenge was a matter of attentiveness. The social/spiritual context of camp helped me pay more attention to my relationship with God. I became reacquainted with Jesus. I went back to doctoral studies shored-up by the summer's fellowship. It gave me bread for the journey over the ensuing ten months at the university. Glory and thanks be to God for the Spirit-filled company that was mine and for the renewal of divine acquaintance over those summers!

Discussion Questions

1. What are the zones of influence in which you are most familiar and comfortable?

2. Are there any mentors or exemplars in your life whose impact you appreciate?

3. What authors or historical figures do you find helpful in your spiritual journey?

4. In what way are you spiritually "in the zone" and how would you describe it?

5. Are you a godly zone in which others might flourish?

six

ACQUAINTING GRACE

I know my sheep, and my sheep know me.

John 14:10

The idea of "getting to know you" in social psychology is called the acquaintance process. The core idea is that complete strangers, when remaining in close proximity and frequent contact with one another, have ample opportunity to become well acquainted. Initially strangers, under conditions of opportunity and motivation various relationships among persons emerge.

The key concepts in the acquaintance process are opportunity and motivation for proximity and frequency of contact based on attraction. When applied to the social/spiritual zone of our lives, it's about "acquainting holiness" and "synergistic sanctification." Both are explored as our growth in Christ is nourished by the company of others. Other persons become God's means of pouring grace into our lives. They are instrumental to our growth beyond mere acquaintance with Christ. They facilitate an increasing intimacy with him. However, that increasing intimacy is contingent on continual exposures to the grace that God provides through the obedient faith of others. It starts with the family.

The family is a person's first immersion in a social ecology, a first zone of others' influence in life. The child becomes acquainted with the mother's voice heard while still in the womb. With birth, the sound of mother's voice has even greater clarity. One's mother is special because she nourishes the baby day and night. Her face and smile become familiar. The presence, voice, and heartbeat of the mother become known and occasions comfort for the child. Her smell becomes familiar.

As the newborn progresses toward toddlerhood, there's a growing acquaintance with other key people in the child's life. As with the mother, so it increasingly is with others in an escalation of the scope of acquaintance and familiarity. A baby grows in intellect, emotions, and in what Wesley described as tempers or what social psychologists call dispositions. This is the ongoing process of a lifetime. It's the social life that characterizes God's plan for us.

In social/spiritual ecologies, we get to know God as the loving Father, not unlike the love of a mother. It's life in the company of others who are obedient to God's desire that we are loved and shaped into the divine likeness. Just as a baby comes into the zone of family life, so God brings us into the sanctified life zones of others beyond the family throughout life's long journey. This is the pattern of social life characterizing our acquaintance with God. These others introduce us to Jesus whose life puts a face on God. In this way, we grow acquainted with our Father God through the Son by the presence of the Holy Spirit exhibited in others.

Natural growth and development bring increased freedom to choose life zones. Our choices determine the social/spiritual integrity and quality of subsequent exposures. In even in the most challenging, toxic, and unhealthy contexts, God can intervene and bring us into the company and influence of healthy others. We become acquainted with others whom we did not seek to know, yet who bring grace, health, wholeness, and holiness into our lives.

This is what God does with parents, extended family, teachers and instructors, friends, mentors, coaches, and others. We may be drawn to them by admiration and curiosity, but the Holy Spirit is at work in them as they come alongside us. Often through one person we meet others and find ourselves becoming acquainted with several others in a shared context of acquaintance. We call this "community," the place where God is at work engaging us in a dynamic, interactive process of acquaintance. Where there is acquaintance we find revelation of God.

Getting Acquainted

The acquaintance process has been scientifically studied in the realm of social psychology.[24] Rather than share the dry content of the studies, allow me to share a personal story that captures the concept and may resonate with your experience.

When I was a first-year student at a Wesleyan-Holiness based, liberal arts college, it took me nearly the first academic year to muster the courage to ask a particular girl out on a date. I spotted twins playing in the college band. One played the oboe, the other the French horn. They were accomplished musicians. More interestingly, they were cute. I discovered that one of them was dating another student. I persevered with the prospect of a date, assuming that the odds were good at least with the twin who was not already spoken for. With only a few weeks left before the summer break, I asked her out and received a favorable response. After two dates, that was the end of that.

I persevered over the summer, trying to keep the nascent relationship alive, but success, according to acquaintance theory, necessarily requires two key things: (1) proximity and (2) frequent contact. Over the summer, I had neither going for me. The twin of interest was working for the summer on the Jersey shore and I was a few hundred miles away lifeguarding at a Christian summer camp just north of Pittsburgh. Moreover, all of my attempts at contact (letters, postcards, phone calls) were totally ignored, so I had absolutely no contact with her. However, the other nice twin would personally respond on every contact attempt. She seemed sweet and was identically cute.

When the next semester started, I learned that the "nice twin" had dropped her boyfriend and showed increasing responsiveness to my attentions. For the next two years, I made it a daily point to pursue the relationship, to get to know this very interesting, bright, cute other twin. We were in the zone, in a full gear of acquaintance by increasing proximity and frequent contact.

I was motivated. I worked my schedule to coincide with hers. I would hustle to meet her after class, to walk her to the next one, even when getting to my next class on time was a challenge. We became acquainted and as increasingly intimate as two souls could at a conservative Christian college. Over time she transformed from being cute to beautiful. Love transforms. At the end of our third academic year, I was "all in," profoundly in love and sold on Irene. I had captured her head, heart, and mind, and she certainly had captured mine. I proposed marriage, and we were married during our fourth academic year.

I realize this narrative may sound like a soap opera, but here's the point. As students together, Irene and I were immersed in the social/spiritual context of our college that made possible a wholesome process of acquaintance. We grew from being strangers to acquaintances, to friends, to increased social and spiritual intimacy, to the loving intimacy of bride and groom, husband and wife, and life-long best friends.

The social/spiritual milieu of the college was significant in this process. The college was a relatively sanctified setting. The community of faith, being a holiness-oriented college, fostered a healthy courtship. While not perfect, the people who made up the college community, the faculty, students, staff, and leadership, were saints in the making. The college was a kind of social/intellectual ecology of holiness promoting a spiritually rich nurturing environment in which to grow our relationship.

My growing love for Irene back then was the same context and process for getting to know and profoundly love God. The acquaintance process was the same for deepening faith, growing in grace, maturing and being spiritually formed, and being perfected in the likeness of Jesus. The process moved head, heart, and life together toward greater fulfillment.

The words of the Apostle Paul in his letter to a young faith community captures the nature of the acquaintance process with God. "Once you were alienated from God and were enemies in your minds because of your evil behavior. But now he has reconciled you by Christ's physical body through death to present you holy in his sight, without blemish and free from accusation if you continue in your faith, not moved from the hope held out in the gospel" (Colossians 1:21-23).

Notice the spiritual progression from alienated, having no relationship, to being reconciled by and in a restored relationship with God, to holiness implying growth in friendship, and finally to being an intimate member of the family of God in the fellowship of all the saints. The journey of acquainting grace looks like this (read from the bottom up):

Intimacy, Infilling, Cleansing

Being Perfected in Christ's likeness

Growth in Grace and Holiness

Restored in Relationship

Redeemed and Reconciled

Alienated from God

The progression does not occur in a spiritual vacuum. Instead, acquainting grace is the active element in the social/spiritual context of dynamic interactive fellowship with God and others.

The reconciliation that Paul mentions implies redemption through more than regret, but first through repentance of sin leading to reconciliation of the relationship. Repentance is occasioned by sufficient acquaintance with God, especially seeing the loving kindness, grace, and the self-giving love in Christ's death on the cross. In such seeing we come to see ourselves as sinners loved by God.

The acquaintance process is God's provision of others to help us come into God's presence through their presence. As we come to know them, we begin to know about God, then know God and His holy love, and in time grow beyond more than mere acquaintance. Their help makes possible an increasingly intimate relationship with God, so intimate that we grasp the magnitude of God's love, and His boundless, full salvation whereby God fills us to the brim with His very self (Ephesians 2:19b).

Acquainting grace does not happen in a vacuum. It unfolds in a social/spiritual context that facilitates awareness of God's identity, presence, and holy love. It happens through the presence of God in the Christian life. It happens when we discover that the love of God is real and is seen in sanctified others who comprise an ecology of holiness. When we see it we want more. When we see it we understand the essence of God.

God is love, pure love. We come to want a life of more, more of God's presence, love, and indwelling in our hearts and lives. We increasingly desire to be filled to the brim and spilling over in self-giving love for others.

Ecologies of Holiness

Earlier I mentioned that an underlying point of this book is that holiness, being filled to the measure of the fullness of God, is both process and encounter that bring us into unity and intimacy with God. It's a developmental process of growing in grace and a crisis experience of encounter, of infilling and cleansing by the Holy Spirit. The process sets the stage for the encounter. Neither happens in a social/spiritual vacuum, but rather in a spiritually ecological context of others.

This process aligns itself with the field known as the ecology of human development. If we take into account the whole person's development, including spiritual transformation, we appreciate that such development is made possible by the Holy Spirit's work channeling God's perfect love through others. It's others, serving together as ecologies of holiness, who comprise the company we keep. They serve God as the means of grace reaching us with His perfect love. By their presence and influence, God fulfills the great desire "that Christ may dwell in our hearts by faith" (Ephesians 3:17).

The Apostle Paul's letter to the Ephesians is for us today. In chapter three he writes from his prayer life with God: "and I pray that you [plural] being rooted and established...." Here Paul is using an ecological, organic metaphor, being rooted and established, like trees in a forest. He is speaking of our spiritual growth in the context of God's love and people. God the Gardener plants the seed, cares for the growth, and facilitates the mature development, often with the help of ecologies of faith communities, the gardens of God's love.

God makes possible the process of acquaintance and being rooted and established in love. By grace we become acquainted with others and through them come to know God personally. This is God's process of acquainting grace. It may lead to becoming rooted and established in love as we grow in our relationships with others. Along the way we are attracted to others, grow to like and love them, and feel fulfilled in the self-giving love we receive and give.

When we speak of getting to know Jesus through ecologies of holiness, we are discussing the characteristics and potential of healthy families, churches as faith communities, workplaces, and community gatherings, healthy universities, colleges, schools, classrooms, summer camps, community centers, athletic teams, hospitals, prisons, and any setting that shapes the lives of people in the likeness of Jesus Christ through acquaintance, friendship, and love.

The tide of social holiness flows with the love and support we experience through the sanctified company we keep. In the words of William Booth, "O boundless [full] salvation, deep ocean of love…."

Acquaintance and the Great Commission

The acquaintance process makes it possible to grow saints. In Matthew 28:18-20 we read Christ's great commission to the eleven disciples: "Go make disciples." The directive is not to make "converts" but *disciples*. When Jesus called the disciples to follow him, it wasn't merely a call to conversion, but a call to help others to go on to grow in acquaintance with God. It was a call to follow Christ in friendship, and eventually in intimacy. Likewise, disciples are to make disciples, to bring others to a knowledge of God.

Jesus directed his disciples to make disciples, followers, by teaching them to obey everything he commanded. They were to be teachers with a particular focus in their obedience. Jesus said to them, "If anyone loves me, he will obey what I command. Then he gave this command to them, "Now remain in my love. If you obey my commands you will remain in my love." The greatest commands are "Love the Lord your God with all your heart and with all your soul and with all you mind and with all your strength" and "Love your neighbor as yourself."

If followers of Jesus are obedient to the call to love and remain, they increasingly become spiritually capable of being obedient to the great commission of making disciples and teaching those disciples from the fruit of their own lives. Lives become lived in the company of Christ. This is what Jesus then promised, "And surely I am with you always." Jesus would perpetually be the company they kept. At Pentecost (Acts 2:1-13) Jesus fulfilled that promise through the history-shaking gift of the Holy Spirit.

A key article of belief in my faith community is, "Continuance in the state of salvation [not a static state, but a dynamic, interactive, interpersonal relationship, a position of solidarity with Christ] depends upon continued obedient faith in Christ." It implies acquaintance leading to an active, progressive relationship with God and with others. Life in Christ by the Spirit is continuing the journey in obedience to everything Jesus commands. Scripture reminds us that if we love him we will obey his directives, starting with the great commandments to profoundly love God and neighbor. Because we remain in his company, obedience becomes not a chore but a joy.

In the sacred space of God's presence, we become like God. God is the company we keep. This is the very heart of social holiness. We are drawn into the intimate life of God the Father, Son, and Holy Spirit. We become privy to the conversations and characteristics of the Trinity. From that privileged position of increasing intimacy, we are restored even more to the beautiful likeness of Christ, the renewed *Imago Dei*. We become energized and equipped, motivated and animated to share the good news of the gospel with others.

Remaining in the company of Christ, we pray that all those with whom we spend time will experience the presence and beauty of Christ in us. We share Christ's company with others. We pray that the love of God in us may be grasped as God's profound love for them. We do it in faith singing these beautiful words of Albert Orsborn:

> Let the beauty of Jesus be seen in me,
> All his wonderful passion and purity,
> O thou Spirit divine, all my nature refine,
> Till the beauty of Jesus be seen in me.

The Social Psychology of Social Holiness

Research into the acquaintance process is a classic line of inquiry in social psychology. It's about the ways that people get to know each other and interact to establish meaningful relationships. It parallels the acquaintance process of how God's presence, identity, and nature become real to us and move us into intimacy with Him. The social nature of interpersonal relations is no surprise since the God of creation designed and built the divine nature into us, passing His social and moral character on to us.

God is pure, perfect love. We are designed in God's image with an interpersonal capacity to be like Him socially and morally, in intellect, heart, and life. Social psychology in many ways is catching up with biblical truths that confirm that we are social and moral beings with innate orientations to each other. Scripture reveals the origin of these inclinations as our Creator. Over years of inquiry in the literature of social psychology, we find a high degree of consensus with Scripture regarding who we are and how we socially and morally function at our best (and worst).

Aristotle said we are "social animals." He was right. Research shows that we are socially inclined from birth, even when in the womb, suggesting the truth of Psalm 149:13-14: "You created my inmost being; you knit me together in my mother's womb. I praise you because I am fearfully and wonderfully made; your works are wonderful, I know that full well."

Child development studies have observed that infants are born with the basics of intuitive ethics, recognizing the difference between kind and unkind actors. Little babies prefer puppets who act kindly.[25] Other researchers have observed the ability of young children to detect when another person needs help, and then is inclined to offer appropriate help.[26] We are both socially and morally wired.

In recent decades, social psychology has produced of tsunami of research findings regarding us as "social animals."[27] The fact is that human thought, emotion, and behavior are strongly influenced by the real, implied, and imagined presence of other people. People want to belong. We seek to be in the presence of others and to interact with others. What we know from the work of social psychologists helps us appreciate the relationship we experience and share with God.

If you were to review a standard undergraduate textbook on social psychology, you would discover a great deal about social factors that especially relate directly to social holiness. For example, the best predictor of whether two people are friends is their sheer proximity (closeness) to each other. That includes not only physical proximity (geographic distance) but functional proximity (frequency of contact). In relationship to others, we become friends with friends who park their car or bicycles near ours, use the same entrances and elevators, frequent the same recreation areas, or sit in church pews near where we usually sit. We tend to like people under these conditions. Proximity brings about exposures and opportunities for interactions that make possible the discovery of similarities and the experience of other's liking and loving.

By mere proximity and contact with others, we form similar attitudes, beliefs, values, and feelings. Just being in close proximity, such as waiting in line or being seated next to someone on a plane, occasions interaction even when there is no reason. Some studies suggest that people affiliate with others for four primary reasons: to obtain positive stimulation, for emotional support, to gain social comparison information, and to receive attention from other people.[28] People seeking to be with others are often seeking acceptance and belonging, approval and liking.

Social psychology explains that we are other-oriented and socially influenced. We seek each other's presence. We do the same with God. Psalms 42:1 says, "As a deer seeks streams of water, so my soul pants for you, O God." Just how and why that is so, under varying conditions with people, are the questions social psychology has sought to empirically explore. The knowledge accrued in social psychological inquiry has progressed beyond "arm chair" social philosophers through empirical inquiry and experimentation. Social psychology has bloomed as a field of science, now fostering an appreciation of the influence that individuals and groups have on others.

The presence and participatory engagement of others is powerful in shaping our character, habits, perceptions, attributions, attitudes, values, judgments, and desires to belong to something greater than oneself. Others increasingly impart something of themselves to us in the process of acquaintance. We participate in their lives as they do in ours, and so reciprocally we become the company we keep.

Intimacy

The Apostle Peter writes that we may "participate in the divine nature" (2 Peter 1:4). Such participation suggests a close relationship, even closer than friendships, romantic engagement, and family. It implies intimacy. Jesus prayed that we may be one with him and the Father (John 17:22-24). One could say that the entire biblical narrative is a relational love story of God seeking a responsive, intimate relationship with humanity, personally and collectively.[29]

We see this in the continual provision of God's grace and our response. The pattern of grace and response describes the pattern of interaction that defines the relationship. Social psychological inquiry goes beyond the study of affiliation, acceptance, and belonging to the study of "close relationships." Some research has been explicit in defining closeness as intimacy and view it as the outcome when people understand, validate, and care for each other, and especially when they are responsive to each other. The greatest attention to closeness in the literature focuses on responsiveness given and received.[30]

Scripture and science provide overlapping wisdom regarding our human nature. The ideas and theories explaining our human-to-human relationships help us understand our primary relationship with God. They illuminate the process of acquaintance with God and others. They work together to move us beyond mere acquaintance into intimacy with God and others. Likewise, the stories, proverbs, and lessons found in the Bible occasion wisdom and insight into the historical narrative of humankind. They reveal the commonalities of personhood between God and ourselves.

The Bible and social psychological research bring a richness and color to our appreciation for the integration of theological and empirical insight. Together they help us understand existing paradigms of social/spiritual engagement.

DISCUSSION QUESTIONS

1. Who comes to mind when you think of someone with whom you've become acquainted? At what stage are you presently getting to know them?

2. Where are you in an acquainting grace process with God?

3. How does your present location in the process correspond with where you are on Barna's ten transitional stops?

4. How would you describe your spiritual ecology presently? Toxic? Healthy? Holy?

5. With whom do you see the God of grace being active in another's life? Do you recognize it in your own life?

seven

WAYS AND MEANS OF GROWING SAINTS

And whatever you do, whether in word or deed,
do it all in the name of the Lord Jesus,
giving thanks to God the Father through him.

Colossians 3:17

God is ready to grow saints in His likeness, holiness. How do we do our part to grow saints? The question addresses the "how" of social holiness. The answer is engagement. Social holiness, being dynamic, interactive, and relational, requires personal engagement with God and, through God's instrumental means of grace, with the company of others.

The company of others makes engagement possible. This includes God's means of grace: the power of small behavior settings; opportunities occasioned by location (proximity and contact with others); the process of becoming increasingly acquainted with others and through others with the Other; opportunities for divine exposures, encounters, reflection, and dialogue with God; and finally the blessing of being held accountable by others, quality assurance of obedient faith along our spiritual journey.

Over the millennia God has used paradigms of social/spiritual engagement to save the lost and grow saints. We see these most clearly and profoundly in the life and ministry of Jesus. But they are evident down through Christian history in the monastic tradition and in the Great Awakenings of the eighteenth and nineteenth centuries. We still see them today in the diversity of John Wesley's Methodist movement and in the missional ministries of Wesley's progeny, saints like The Salvation Army's William and Catherine Booth, Free Methodism's B. T. Roberts, Asbury's E. Stanley Jones and John Wesley Hughes, the Church of God's (Anderson) Daniel Sidney Warner, the Church of the Nazarene's Phineas F. Bresee and Joseph Pomeroy Whidney, the Foursquare Church's Aimee Semple McPherson, the Christian Missionary Alliance's A. B. Simpson, and the Wesleyan Church's Orange Scott.[31]

The overarching framework of Divine-human engagement throughout both the Old and New Testaments is divine grace and human response. God's grace comes first at every step of the journey from sin and darkness to sanctification and great light. God acts by offering grace and waits for response. Through common paradigms of engagement, God deploys means by which the provision of grace anticipates our response. While God gives us the freedom not to respond, to ignore the many forms in which grace is offered, the paradigms of engagement are compelling and often effective.

Our response to God's grace is the work we do in the dynamic relationship of growing in divine grace. That work is obedient faith that makes possible continual forward movement toward holiness. That continuing synergism is a kind of co-operant grace as we cooperate with the Holy Spirit in our restoration and formation into the likeness of Jesus. Paul puts it this way: "Work out your salvation" (a full salvation) "with fear and trembling, for it is God who works in you to will and to do according to his good purpose" (Philippians 2:12).

Means of Grace

The primary path of engagement is John Wesley's framework of activities that typically convey God's grace. Our day by day walk in the Christian life leading to transformation is helped by practices that Wesley called "the means of grace." They are the activities by which the Holy Spirit engages and leads us to experience God's presence and appreciate His identity. Through our participation in the means of grace, God spiritually forms and transforms us into His likeness.

Christian growth in grace accrues through the practice of the means of grace. They open us to experience God's love and afford us ways of participating in the life of the Trinity. Diane Leclerc writes, "Participating in the means of grace serves to remind us that all we do, all we are, and all we become is only possible through the grace of God within us through the presence of the Holy Spirit.... Sometimes such participation looks like discipline. But it is never our discipline alone that creates and maintains our Christ-like character."[32]

The means of grace are similar to Richard Foster's spiritual disciplines. The focus is on the means God provides rather than the disciplines we engage on our own. Wesley conceived of the means of grace in three categories: general, prudential, and instituted (particular). By general means of grace, he meant universal obedience and keeping the commandments; watching as an intentional act of seeking God, looking for His activity in the world; denying one's self; setting aside distractions and attractions of the culture that tend to block the channel of God's grace; daily taking up one's cross through enduring hardships and suffering, thus drawing closer to God and divine purposes; and exercising the presence of God by directly communing with God throughout the day.

By prudential means of grace, Wesley meant regular acts (rules) of holy living pursued with the participation of others, such as small group fellowship of support and accountability, "watching over one another in love," prayer meetings, covenant services, and other gatherings with God's people, doing all the good one can and doing no harm, visiting the sick and hopeless as agents of God's mercy, and reading devotional, edifying literature.

By instituted (particular) means of grace, Wesley meant prayer, both private and corporate, and searching the Scriptures, both essential to transformation, fasting and abstinence, Christian "conference" and conversation about God's grace in thanks, praise, encouragement, and mutual support, and the Lord's supper as a sacrament, an outward sign of an inward grace.

Another way Wesley organized the idea of God's means of grace was in direct relationship to Christ's Great Commandments to love the Lord with all our mind, heart, soul, and strength, and to love our neighbor as ourselves. He understood that acts of piety help us appreciate God's presence and identity. They are the means by which we engage in loving God. Acts of mercy help us see Jesus in others as we love, serve, and identify with our neighbor. The means of grace are effective on a private basis, but often more so in the company of others, especially in the context of small behavior settings. This is the nature of social holiness.

WELSEY'S MEANS OF GRACE

ACTS OF PIETY	ACTS OF MERCY
Public prayer	Feeding the hungry
Family prayer	Clothing the naked
Praying in one's closet	Hospitable to the stranger (alien)

Receiving the Lord's Supper	Visiting those in prison and sick
Searching the Scriptures by hearing, reading, meditating	Instruct the ignorant
Fasting	Awaken those stupefied in sin
Abstinence	Quicken the lukewarm
Partaking of the Lord's Supper[33]	Confirm the wavering & tempted

Small Behavior Settings

The second paradigm is small behavior settings. Our lives consist of a stream of movements through small behavior settings: families, nurseries and day cares, schools, camper cabins, band practices, scouting programs, study groups in college, employment in small business, Bible studies, Sunday school classes, fellowship groups, sports teams, book clubs, and so on. Small behavior settings also include therapy groups, support groups, focus groups, and informal coffee or breakfast klatches, and inner circles.

Christ's ministry often engaged small behavior settings. As a member of the Godhead, Jesus belongs to the inner circle of three divine persons we call the Trinity. During his ministry, he formed an inner circle of three, then the twelve, and then a large community of disciples who followed his teaching and healing ministry. John Wesley discovered the power of small groups (class meetings and bands) well before social psychologists did. They were the primary way Methodists and others in his day grew in grace and became saints.

Small behavior settings, not unlike Wesley's class meetings and bands, are superior to large ones. Small groups offer more opportunities for participation, have a quicker pace of acquaintance, and sustain involvement of each member at a higher level than large groups. They have a greater level of familiarity and comfort among members and result in more trust in, responsibility for, and confidentiality among participants. Small high schools often produce a stronger population of graduates proportionately than large schools. Small colleges and universities are often superior in delivering quality undergraduate education than large, public universities.

The genius of John Wesley lay not only in his balanced, orthodox theology, but also in his practical orthopraxy of Christian life in small gatherings. His small groups were a *ecclesiolae in ecclesia* (little churches in the big church) similar to the dominant structure of the church in the earliest years of the Christian faith.

Today social psychologists call Wesley's class meetings and bands by another name, small behavior settings. In those settings, every member has an opportunity to be heard, share, listen, and grow within the support and affirmation of others. Wesley's class meetings and bands were healthy, growth-promoting innovations and interventions. They were small enough (ten to twelve persons in class meetings and smaller in bands) to be interactive and dynamic for everyone.

In their interactive engagement, Wesley's small, peer-driven groups brokered spiritual nutrients of grace for every member, including the reading of Scripture, prayer, testimonies, confessions, repentance, reconciliation, and reports of service opportunities to meet the needs of members and others outside the group. No member was ignored. No one was left out. Everyone was supported. Each one supported every other one. Everyone was held accountable for spiritual progress.

The small class-meeting groups provided the grace of accountability as social/spiritual ecologies of learning, support, transparency, and discipline occasioned through the company of others. When the small groups were not healthy, supportive, and taken seriously in their accountability, Wesley corrected or disbanded them.

Wesley's small groups had a structure that new Christians especially needed. They had rules that promoted frequent contact face to face, helped by meeting together close to home. They had a measure of hospitality by meeting in a member's home and at a set time. They were kept small and engaged the means of grace in singing, the reading of Scripture, prayer, and testimonies about spiritual victories and defeats in the past week. Through the engagement of God's means of grace, small Wesleyan behavior settings grew saints.

This is not the normative scene in many church small groups today. Overwhelmingly, fellowship groups, Bible studies, and small group prayer meetings offer little or no accountability, no practical support of tough love, little or no responsibility for each other in staying the course of faithful obedience.

Location

A third paradigm of engagement is location. In the real estate business, they say that the three most important words are location, location, location. The Bible says something about location as proximity. You may recall the story in Jeremiah underscoring the optimal location for the people of Israel in relation to God. It was all about the importance of proximity, staying close to God. They were to be so close as to cling to the heart of God, as close as a belt or sash clings around the waist of man, and for good reason. Without continual, obedient faith, remaining close to the heart of God, they drifted, became distant, and in time ruined, worthless, and beyond restoration of beauty, functional value, or glory to God. The word of the Lord came to Jeremiah saying:

> In the same way I will ruin the pride of Judah and the great pride of Jerusalem. These wicked people, who refuse to listen to my words, who follow the stubbornness of their hearts and go after other gods to serve and worship them, will be like this belt—completely

useless. For as the belt is bound around a man's waist, so I bound the whole house of Judah to me… to be my people for my renown, and praise and honor. But they have not listened. (Jeremiah 13:11)

What's going on in this story? What went wrong? God is making it clear that people placed themselves in the wrong location, a poisonous context, a toxic ecology. God's people were to remain in close proximity to God.

We were made for fellowship with God and with each other, to remain in the company of God, close to His heart. "He has raised up for his people a horn, the praise of all his saints… the people close to his heart" (Psalms 148:14). Likewise, the prophet Isaiah reports that God "tends his flock like a shepherd; He gathers his lambs in his arms and carries them close to his heart; He gently leads those who have young" (Isaiah 40:11). James encourages our location in relationship to God, "Draw near to God and he will draw near to you" (James 4:8).

Location in God's company makes possible the acquaintance process discussed earlier. Since we were in our mother's womb, we've been at some point along a journey of acquaintance with God. Like an unborn baby comes to recognize the mother's heartbeat and voice, we develop friends, come to know others. As they become familiar to us and we become comfortable and trusting of them, we move to knowing them well, even to interpersonal intimacy of heart and soul.

Our journey of salvation is the same. It's God's plan for us to journey from the uttermost of sin and darkness far from God to the uttermost of holiness, the likeness of Jesus Christ, in intimacy with the fullness of God. It's a journey of engagement with God in an escalating process of drawing near to the divine heart. It's a journey along the path of "acquainting grace." In the classic words of Cleland McAfee,

There is a place of quiet rest, near to the heart of God,
A place where sin cannot molest, near to the heart of God.
O Jesus, blest redeemer, Sent from the heart of God,
Hold us who wait before thee, Near to the heart of God.

Acquaintance

The fourth paradigm of engagement is the acquaintance process. Recall how I met, became acquainted with, and finally married Irene. At first there was no relationship. The acquaintance process moved forward from friendship to intimacy of heart and soul. We were engaged and married by the time we graduated from college. The rest is history. We've lived together for over forty-eight years, fulfilling vows we took way back then.

In reflection about our acquaintance journey, our experience squares with studies in social psychology on the importance of opportunities for forming relationships through physical proximity[34] and exposures.[35] Continuing proximity, contact, and exposures will occasion familiarity, comfort, and liking. Likewise, immediacy in responsiveness to the other can indicate an open, friendly, interested, and pleasant interpersonal disposition, as may smiling, attentive facial expressions, and appropriate interpersonal distance, eye contact, and open body position.

This was our experience. At first Irene and I knew nothing about each other. I had no idea that my beloved even existed. Then I knew more and more about her through growing stages of acquaintance. We became friends and then more than friends. I found myself moving to a higher level of commitment and soul-mate intimacy. We progressed from being strangers, to acquaintances, and on to a close relationship and commitment that transformed into covenant of heart and soul in holy matrimony. Thanks be to God!

It's the same process of holy acquaintance with God. We move from the totally unknown, to knowing about God, then knowing that God is present. With more exposures, we see God more clearly in Jesus Christ's life, ministry, suffering, death, and resurrection. We recognize God in His demonstrative love, pure, self-giving, self-suffering, self-sacrificing, other-oriented love. Our heart's desire comes to acknowledge who God is, to accept God's love and sacrifice on the cross for us, to understand God's forgiveness, saving promises, and desire that we be in divine company throughout life's journey and beyond.

This increasing acquaintance leads to our growing desire to move forward, with the help of others, from being God's friend to being intimate, filled with His fullness, cleansed from all sin, and transformed into His likeness. God's plan for us is to experience acquainting holiness. When Jesus said "I am the way," we may interpret him to mean an acquaintance *process* that leads to loving intimacy, covenant, full salvation, and an unimaginable, profound love of God and others.

This pathway of growing acquaintance and intimacy mirrors Wesley's *via salutis* of prevenient, justifying, sanctifying, and glorifying grace. It hits all of George Barna's transformational stops. For The Salvation Army, it's progressing through the cascading articles of faith that comprise its eleven doctrines. They too mirror Wesley's *via salutis*.[36]

As the divine Trinity, God is a social being who creates us as social beings in the divine image. God transforms us toward holiness by using the company and ministry of others. God, the Other, as the Holy Spirit, moves in and through others for our salvation, and moves in and through us as we are transformed and participate in the salvation of others. God does this through the acquaintance process.

God helps us see life in the light of who God is, who we are, and who we can become. We grasp the inestimable magnitude of God's love for us with a knowledge that surpasses knowledge. The knowledge we gain is knowledge not only of our intellect but of our passion.

This knowledge of both head and heart compels our life toward the likeness of Jesus Christ, transformed as we walk in the Spirit.

Acquainting Holiness Transforms

Acquainting holiness transforms as we experience an ongoing series of daily exposures to God's grace and as God calls us continually to respond in worship, witness, and work. Our relationship with God follows an interactive pattern of God's grace and our response, God's love and our love of God and others in return. This is what Wesley meant by the efficacy of the means of grace, the ways and means by which we are exposed to the presence, identity, and love of God.

Where there are such exposures in times and settings of prayer, Scripture, fellowship, testimony, fasting, confession, repentance, and other means of grace, we will find ourselves reflecting on God's grace, dialoguing with God in prayer, and encountering the presence and ministry of the Holy Spirit. Such actions characterize a transforming ecology of holiness.

Without reflection, there is less or little impact of exposures. Through reflection and dialogue we hear God more clearly and the Holy Spirit engages us and helps us along the journey, using the company of others to transform us in progressive sanctification. We are enabled to move beyond mere acquaintance and friendship with Jesus to maturity and purity of heart and life.

Social holiness provides opportunities for engagement with God personally and through others of like hearts and minds. Being in their presence, we find ourselves in the presence of God. Hearing their thoughts, listening to their thanks, praise, and prayers, being loved and listened to draws us into friendship with others beyond mere acquaintance. We find ourselves in a wholesome, healthy context, a social-spiritual ecology where we are affirmed, loved, and challenged to discover our best selves.

In the ecology of the Spirit, we are drawn into the awareness of and engagement with the Spirit. We encounter the heart and mind of Christ (Philippians 2:5). It is a transformational journey of acquainting holiness in which, amidst all the exposures, reflections, and dialogues, we encounter God. Some encounters are illumination, some compassion, and some conviction leading to a holy discontent. Holy discontent is a good step (or better yet, a good "stop"—see the Barna study). It means that the Holy Spirit is prodding and poking our conscience when our will is holding us back from God's will. It also means that, as we are being fulfilled by God's love and presence, we begin yearning for more. There's always more.

In the pursuit of the available more, we are faced with the needed decision of submission and surrender. We realize that, in the context of the love of others and through others the love of God, it's safe to submit and surrender to God's will and desire. In this context, God makes possible an infilling of the Holy Spirit and the cleansing of our hearts and lives. This is the *telos* (aim, goal, end, purpose) of entire sanctification (Ephesians 3:19b). It's God's filling, cleansing, and empowerment of us for service to God's glory (Ephesians 3:20-21).

DISCUSSION QUESTIONS

1. Are you in a small behavior setting where you can grow to be more acquainted with God, with who he is, and with his love for you?

2. What are the means of grace that you find most helpful in your spiritual journey and transformation? Are they both acts of piety and acts of mercy?

3. Would you say that you are in social/spiritual settings with others that are transformative and help you grow into the likeness of Christ Jesus? After reflection, explain?

4. Where are you now in your journey of acquainting holiness toward mature acquaintance with God?

5. In what ways and with whose company are you pursuing spiritual maturity and purity of heart to be like Jesus?

eight

ACCOUNTABILITY

Speaking the truth in love.

Ephesians 4: 15

The fourth paradigm of engagement, accountability, cannot be emphasized enough. Growing saints requires small, socially spiritual settings of support and accountability not limited to small group Bible studies, prayer meetings, recovery groups, book clubs, cooking classes, sports programs, and missional tourism to other countries. Such groups provide social life and opportunities of support, but often lack engagement with matters of ethical and spiritual accountability.

Accountability involves caring enough about others to go deeper, below the mere surface of social life to true fellowship. The church is full of social life, not fellowship in the biblical sense. Fellowship always brings God, as one or more of the Trinity, into the equation through thanks, praise, prayer, testimony, or by introducing others to means of grace. Fellowship honors the presence of God and at its best is spiritually fulfilling. It brings the light and love of Jesus into relationships. It occasions spiritual growth and fulfillment at every opportunity.

Social life, on the other hand, is at best enjoyable interpersonal interaction void of spiritual fulfillment and accountability. Making disciples requires accountability in the form of feedback and self-evaluation with the help of others. Its focus is progress or failure in obedient faith. Accountability is part of deep, meaningful fellowship between people who truly care about each other and their deepening relationships with God.

Accountability is a preventive measure holding sin in check. It's a spiritual prophylactic. Sin is a shortfall in every Christian's life. Temptation and sins of commission or omission are always real possibilities. No one is immune from sin. It undercuts the vitality of our relationship with God. It interrupts growing in grace and increasing in Christ-likeness. Accountability for sin speaks the truth in love. Where there is sin, there is need for repentance.

When sin is left unaddressed, faith dissipates. Sin damages sacred relationships with God and others and weakens our capacity for love. Being held accountable for sin by others is a check against continuing sin. Accountability safeguards the integrity of the relationship to God. It often is the missing ingredient in the equation of discipleship moving toward holiness.

It's a cliché, but true; accountability is tough love. It's the bold love of others, firm and transparent enough to confront in kindness when sin undercuts a life meant to honor God. True accountability occasions frequent reflection on how well or poorly life in Christ is going. It asks us to think about anything in our recent life that would be an embarrassment or disappointment if others we most admire and respect were to know. The fact that God knows ought to be enough.

Many who profess new life in Jesus Christ have little or no socially spiritual context of accountability. As a result, they go on living in sin. They enjoy all the benefits of church-based social life, but continue devoid of true fellowship and the tough love of accountability.

I recall my father-in-law, pastor of a large church in the Wesleyan Holiness tradition. He moved on to a new pulpit and new conference. The church he left was more of a social club than a serious faith community. The church softball league and the post-worship potluck meals were more of a priority than small accountability groups. He didn't want to preside over a social club where the presence of Christ was not an interest and where persons were not seriously in love with God and living in obedient faith.

The congregation my father-in-law left had entertaining worship and interesting Bible studies, but little or no discipleship, no Methodist ethos of holiness, no response to sanctified preaching, no mutual support and accountability for each other's growth in grace and holiness. The church was in a spiritual rut, an early grave. Whatever ember of fire in conscience and holy discontent there may have been, no one tended to it other than the pastor. After years of frustration and fatigue, and with ten years left until retirement, he moved on.

The people in the former pastorate were disinterested in the practice of shared support and accountability toward spiritual formation and progress. Instead, they were participants in the social life of a church that reflected secular culture. In contrast, the people in the new pastorate reflected a balance of mutual support and accountability. They shared a communal desire for more fellowship and a deeper life. They embraced their brokenness. Their holy discontent was based on a healthy desire to grow in grace and respond to God as disciples and followers of Christ.

Social holiness is most effective when socially spiritual contexts of discipleship grow saints through strong dimensions of fellowship, solidarity, support, and mutual accountability. An essential part of the benefit is holding each other accountable, keeping each other on the path as Christ's faithful followers. Accountability is an exercise in mutual stewardship. Each individual is helped to reflect on the challenges, shortfalls, and opportunities of remaining faithful in pursuit of continual growth in grace and holiness.

This is especially true in the early months and years of coming to faith when the problem of temptation and sin is most challenging. Old habits remain. New distractions arise. The tough love of others willing to ask the hard questions about faith and spiritual progress provides a measure of accountability to each one along the way.

Accountability must be intentional and have structure. In John Wesley's small groups of support and accountability the structure made possible a practice that followed his theology of acquainting grace. As with Wesley, by the routine of meeting together regularly for opportunities to share struggles of the past week and testimonies of faithfulness, set structure and process help to encourage, lift us up, and grow us together. By nurturing awareness of the Spirit's presence in each other's lives, we become intentionally accountable and stronger together.

Wesley's Way

John Wesley was an enthusiast for small groups of accountability. His class meetings saw to it that participants stayed the course, continued in Christ, rooted, built up, and strengthened in the faith (Colossians 2: 6-7).

David L. Watson writes about small-group accountability seen in the early Methodist class meetings of his day (1807). Each class met once a week to give advice, reproof, or encouragement as needed, to bear burdens and care for each another.[37] "Speaking the truth in love, we will in all things grow up into Him in all things, who is the Head, even Christ" (Ephesians 4:15, TNIV).

Watson notes a description of a class meeting written in 1805 by Joseph Nightingale in his *Portrait of Methodism*. The leader of the class meeting investigates the state of every soul present after baring his own: "Well sister, or well brother, how do you find the state of your soul this evening?" The member proceeds to respond with a general recapitulation of what has passed in the mind during the week. Advice, correction, reproof, and consolation, are then given. Everyone receives "a portion of meat in due season."

This structure of the weekly event worked to keep group members accountable in their spiritual journey. In the company of others pursuing holiness, the early class meetings provided a social context where members could stay the course of being saved and encouraged to continue the journey to the uttermost of holiness. They were helped in their salvation to avoid recidivism, the continual fall into the depths of old sinful habits and desires.

Class meetings as small behavior settings were not intended to be passive. By being small, usually eight to ten members, they pulled group members into participation. It's difficult to hide when a group member is one of only a few. The rules called first for every member to be given time and attention in contributing to the process of sharing and caring. The purpose was to promote behavior, activity, and engagement toward spiritual formation and growth.

The small size promoted more opportunity for personal disclosure, familiarity with all members, deepened trust, mutual openness, and a comfort level for all. It made possible a bonding among members. People were free to be themselves and trust each other. All the paradigms of engagement worked together to promote movement toward the goals for which the groups were established. Used by God, they were effective in assisting spiritual growth and transformation.

As in Wesley's day, our God seeks to reveal, minister, enable growth. By His grace often at work in and through others, God shapes us into the divine likeness and fills us to the brim with the Holy Spirit. We are engaged in a number of ways (paradigms) that work together to reveal the truth of God's existence, nature, identity, love for us, and great desire for our holy future.

Paradigms of engagement are at the center of social holiness. Together they help make ecologies of holiness work as God's socially spiritual incubators and greenhouses of holiness.

Obedient Faith and Accountability

The matter of obedience and accountability is so important that it merits more commentary. Obedience is God's litmus test for love. In the beginning, the Garden of Eden was glorious. It only took one act of disobedience to spoil the intimacy Adam and Eve enjoyed in the presence of God. They were immersed in the perfect social/spiritual context of happiness and holiness. God blessed them from the very beginning.

Nevertheless, those first people chose to disobey God's one simple command. By the exercise of their will, they disobeyed. Their paradise was poisoned. Their sin was toxic. Disobedience occasioned separation from God and ultimately their death. God held them accountable for sin and does the same with us. But by grace and loving kindness, God provided an antidote for sin and still does the same for us.

We know the story of Christ's redemption, God's gift of reconciliation and restoration to holiness. God's provision of salvation from sin and eternal punishment is well beyond what we deserve. But, thanks be to God, grace makes possible our sanctification, purity of heart and life, and restoration according to God's original plan for creation. Then God goes further still, inviting us to participate in the redemptive, reconciling, restorative work of salvation for all humankind. By dwelling in us, God uses our presence to convey to the world the divine presence in the world. We become

a spiritual ecology of God's love, even the tough love of accountability in the service of obedient faith.

Socially, relationally, interpersonally, spiritual ecologies promote accountability. They promote a growing faith, a fidelity
to one's relationship with God. The necessity is spelled out in
an old hymn:

> *Prone to wander, Lord I feel it,*
> *Prone to leave the God I love,*
> *Here's my heart, O take and seal it,*
> *Seal it for Thy courts above.*

New believers are especially prone to wander and ignore God's
grace and love. They wander off the path, distracted, enticed, and
conflicted by their own will. They come a good way in their journey, discipled through the love and grace of God that come first
and lead to faith and salvation. But then, as new babes in Christ
Jesus, they are prone to engage old habits of the heart, old desires,
and old dispositions and tempers that lead back into sin. They need
help staying on course with Christ, on the way of salvation, the
way forward.

Avoiding a diversion down the path of temptation and back to
the toxicity of sin, the way forward with Christ requires obedient
faith. For many new Christians, their disobedience shatters their
relationship with God. Jesus said that if a person remains in him
and he in them, they will bear much fruit; if not, then they will
not. Obedient faith is more readily made possible in a spiritually
supportive and healthy ecology of holiness, the company of sanctified others.

In my own faith community there is an article of faith that
states, "Continuance in a state of salvation depends upon continued obedient faith in Christ." In this we find four truths about
salvation:

1. Salvation is not a static relationship. It is a dynamic, interactive, and synergistic love relationship with Jesus Christ, a journey by God's continuing grace that takes us from the uttermost extremes of sin to the uttermost privilege of holiness and transformation.

2. Its continuance toward full salvation is contingent on our love for God demonstrated by our faithful, consistent obedience to divine direction.

3. Such a state of full salvation is one of movement forward to fulfill God's purposes and plan for our restoration, sanctification, and participation in God's divine nature and Kingdom, all to his glory.

4. As God uses others to bring salvation from sin to us, the forward movement of continuing, full salvation is our progressive and entire sanctification. This often comes to us from God by way of others who comprise the socially spiritual ecologies of holiness. Continuance in a state of salvation is staying the course and pursuing forward advance in holiness by continuing engagement in social/spiritual contexts of holiness that God provides in the company we keep.

Socially spiritual contexts may provide powerfully effective accountability structures and opportunities that support obedient faith. In the relational milieu of sanctified others, we find the support that sustains the faith journey. This is especially true in the context of small accountability groups. In the company of mature others, new Christians in Wesley's time found support and help with their faith journey. Along the journey, a supportive ecology of the Spirit engaged them so that they could continue on the way of a full salvation. May it be so today.

Support and Accountability

For many, staying on the path of change and commitment is an overwhelming struggle possible only with the help of others. In 1980-1981 The Salvation Army operated eight mental health and addiction treatment programs on the Island of Oahu. One program was the Women's Way, a residential program that worked exceptionally well with addicted women and their children. It used several of the paradigms of engagement already discussed.[38] Its aim was to restore women and their children physically, socially, and spiritually to health and help them sustain the progress they achieved.

Women's Way was the first program of its kind in the nation. Women who otherwise would have been sentenced to prison were diverted from the criminal justice system into residential addiction treatment that permitted them to bring their children with them. When they entered the program, nearly every woman had suffered a life of abuse and bondage to drugs, prostitution, and sexual exploitation. Their children, pre-natal to teens, came as victims of neglect. The support of the program was only temporary, lasting nine to twelve months. It was artificial in not being the reality in which they would live for the remainder of their lives. Eventually the women had to re-enter the real world. Then, depending on the decisions they made and the company they chose to keep, they could fall back into the stranglehold of addiction or go forward into a new life.

A major principle of the program was to support the women and their kids until eventually they became established in a healthy, positive social and spiritual context that would continue the process of healing and lead to complete restoration. This included avoiding the old life, the old neighborhood, and former toxic friends.

It meant the necessity of keeping company with those who were healthy, loving, kind, generous, and affirming rather than others who were toxic, exploitive, and dangerous. The company they were to keep going forward would have to be supportive in many ways, especially in accountability. The combination of compassionate support and strong accountability would be necessary for recovery and personal restoration.

At the heart of recovery and restoration was an immersion into Christian faith communities. In addition to the Army's church settings, by God's grace there were grace-filled, Bible-believing fellowships on Oahu ready and willing to embrace the women and their children, to love, support and strengthen them in their faith. The social/spiritual ecology of the churches helped them discover Jesus and accept his loving embrace. They nurtured and strengthened their faith and helped them see the esteem that God had for them.

The glory of God was revealed in the love of others and was their glory as well. From the love and care of others, the recovering women would receive the encouragement and strength necessary for healing. In the company of others they found the presence and love of God. For those who did not fall back but continued going forward with the social and spiritual support and accountability of others, their journey took them from the trash bins of life to a new life of hope and promise. God's company was their glory and strength.

Women's Way has never been fully successful, of course. All programs of its kind experience recidivism. Many women over the years fell back into addiction. Too often faith communities stigmatize recovering persons who are vulnerable in their faith journey and need the very support churches and faith fellowships may offer as alternatives to recidivism. But, overall, the story of Women's Way may be considered a success.

While many people define social holiness as social service, social holiness is far more. At the heart of social holiness is God's essence, the presence of Jesus through the Spirit in the social/spiritual life of all those who make up the ecology of a particular setting. If it were only social service, it would be form without essence. It would lack the holy love of God, the essential attribute of holiness. Without love, social services may do much good, but not the most good possible.

The Salvation Army's Women's Way program is now in its thirty-eighth year of serving women and children. Although it has been partially funded by the state, its social holiness nature is not a public policy. The women liberated from addiction were recovered and restored to new life centered in Christ by the Spirit-filled, instrumental company of others. At its core, the essence of Women's Way is the love of Jesus Christ through the means of grace provided by others. Women's Way is a kind of Potter's wheel that God engages to reshape broken lives and restore their function and beauty. This is social holiness. Glory to God!

Contemporary Structures of Accountability

Not everyone needs a highly structured treatment program like Women's Way or Alcoholics Anonymous. But everyone is prone to wander and can benefit by the support provided by a variation on John Wesley's class meetings and bands. Prudence suggests that the form of such groups vary in size and honor the diversity of education, income, gender, or other demographic characteristics of its members. A group's essence ought to honor God in seeking holiness and be transparent, trustful, encouraging, and committed to being spiritually supportive and accountable by speaking the truth in love.

New group forms are now possible. In an age of the internet and social media, it's possible that small groups of support and accountability can link members across miles, cultures, and boundaries once thought impossible.

DISCUSSION QUESTIONS

1. Are there times in your life when you've been prone to wander from your walk with Christ? Are there times when faith seems to dissipate?

2. How would you define spiritual accountability and what does it look like in your life?

3. Of all the groups in which you participate, which ones are merely social in nature and which ones provide spiritual fellowship and accountability?

4. Would you describe your spiritual life in Jesus Christ as static or dynamic? If static, what can you do about it? If dynamic, what is the evidence?

5. To whom do you turn and trust to speak the truth in love regarding your spiritual growth? Who holds you accountable in your Christian life?

6. Do you know of or belong to a small group that functions through social media for the purpose of support and accountability?

nine

THE POTTER'S WHEEL

We are the clay. You are the potter.
We are all the work of your hand.

Isaiah 64:8 TNIV

The metaphor of God the Potter and we the clay has simplicity and clarity. It's profound in its implications. In the plural voice of the Isaiah passage, "We are the clay." It acknowledges God's work. God is not passive but actively involved in shaping our lives as individuals and as a people into something beautiful and functional.

Who's not played with clay as a child? Metaphors are powerful when captured by objects that are common and accessible. Vases, bowls, pitchers, saucers, cups, and other forms of pottery were certainly common in Isaiah's day, as were the potters who made them in the smallest of villages.

I still have a vase I bought in Beijing, China, in 1984. It's made of clay with a porcelain finish. The potter shaped it to be both functional and beautiful. It has value in its simplicity and beauty and brings back memories of my first trip to China. It also reminds me of another verse in the Bible about the Potter and the clay: "Then the word of the Lord came to me: O house of Israel. Can I not do with you as the potter does, declares the Lord? Like clay in the hand of the potter, so are you in my hand" (Jeremiah 18:5-6).

Clay on the Potter's Wheel

The Bible is God's Living Word. In the days of Isaiah and Jeremiah the Word had meaning and purpose. It still does today. The Apostle Paul echoed the potter passages when he wrote, "We are God's handiwork, created in Christ Jesus to do good works" (Ephesians 2:10 TNIV).

The Bible is filled with metaphors. God is the Potter who takes the clay of our lives and shapes us into vessels of holiness. We are filled to the brim with the divine essence, pure love. God loves us and loves to shape us for service to others and ultimately for His glory.

> Spirit of the Living God, fall afresh on me.
> Spirit of the Living God, fall fresh on me.
> *Break me, melt me, mold me, fill me.*
> Spirit of the Living God, fall fresh on me.

The idea of God the Potter and we the clay implies that the Holy Spirit breaks us with conviction and holy discontent, moves us to surrender and submission, shapes the clay of our lives to be functional and beautiful, and fills us to the brim with Himself. Only recently has another dimension of this metaphor come to mind. It resonates with social holiness. It's the idea that God the Potter often calls others to partner with him in the creative process of spiritual formation.

God engages others in the instrumental role of service and deploys them in the work of shaping the clay of our lives. God is the ultimate artist who can create anything on His own, but chooses to engage others in ways that are instrumental in the work of our spiritual formation. In this way, social and relational contexts comprised of others are the wheels of God the Potter. Who and what are the Potter's wheels?

The Potter's wheel can be many things. In the presence of sanctified others, we find ourselves in the presence of Christ. In the helping hands of others, we feel the hands of Christ on the clay of our lives. The Potter's wheel may be found where the love of Christ compels the transforming love and compassion of others in families, schools, summer camps, community centers, churches, youth groups, coffee shop gatherings, colleges and universities, church fellowships, book clubs, sports teams, summer camps, support groups, and neighbors. The family may be the most influential of all the Potter's wheels, especially at particular stages of a person's life.

Families. It's a truism that families can be contexts of health or toxicity. Ideally family contexts are expressions of perfect love after the likeness of the Trinity. At their best, they are relational contexts of self-giving love, affirmation, mutual support, trust and unity. This is not surprising when we understand the importance of family to God and how we are adopted into God's family as daughters and sons.

Throughout Scripture, God uses metaphors of family and family life to describe His desire and purpose for us.[39] We see this when Moses obeys God's call to liberate the descendants of Abraham from Egyptian bondage. Moses serves as a Potter's wheel as God begins to shape the future of Israel. In Psalm 2:3-4 we read God's declaration, "I have installed my King on Zion," saying, "You are my Son; today I have become your father." The mention of David as both King and Son, and God as Father, is clearly both regal and familial. we see in 2 Samuel 7:14 a similar double promise and prophecy. God says to David regarding his son Solomon, "I will be his father and he will be my son."

This messianic prophecy returns upon Christ's entry into Jerusalem with the crowd chanting "Hosanna to the Son of David. Blessed is the king who comes in the name of the Lord!" (Matthew 21:9, Luke 19:38). David and Jesus share a special status. While there is only one Messiah, in Scripture both are called God's son. Yet, through the blood of Jesus Christ, all children of men who believe in Christ and accept him as Lord and Savior become children of God. All may pray the prayer Christ taught, "Our Father...."

From the beginning, God's design was that every person come into the world with a father and mother. Within the family our identities as sons and daughters are established. Our moral and ethical orientation to parents, siblings, and progeny are established. The family is a sanctuary promoting life and nurturing development. In the family the character of father and mother should be derived from the character of God the Father, the one who offers the most profound, intimate relationship of perfect love. Parents become the first company children keep and they can pass the perfect love of God to their children over a lifetime.

Ideally, the family is an ecology of God's love, a Potter's wheel by which the intimate influence of family shapes the clay, the identity and character of the children. It's the bedrock of grace leading a child to holiness later in life in the spirit of Proverbs 22:6, "Train-up a child in the way he should go, and when he is old, he will not depart from it" (KJV).

My parents raised six children in a Wesleyan social/spiritual milieu of holiness. At first I didn't know how special my family was. I just sensed the beauty of holiness in the climate of my family and church settings. I felt safe, loved, and good about life. I had no words for it as a child, but I remember that the holiness of others smelled something like fresh baked bread wafting in the air, more of a comfort and warmth than a way of life. I was born into such a context, awakening one day to discover what it really was in contrast to other social and spiritual contexts that are tragically void of holy love.

In the ecology of the family, habits of the heart are formed. This is the context where formative means of grace (acts of piety and mercy) were practiced in my presence. I eventually learned that it is in the family where the presence and identity of God first comes into a child's awareness, where a personal faith relationship with Christ is formed, where intimacy with God is made possible. Family is where curiosity and questions of faith arise and are answered, where a thirst for knowledge of God can be explored and addressed. God shapes the heart and uses the family as a powerful Potter's wheel shaping a child's heart and life into the likeness of Jesus.

Special Schools for Special Needs. In the mountains of eastern Kentucky is a remarkable place for young people called Oakdale School. It's a Christian school where there's a healthy mix of teens who have special social, emotional, and spiritual needs and others who do not. The teachers and staff are committed to the mission of the school. It's a wholesome setting where the love of Christ Jesus brings healing and transformation to all its students.

This school is especially effective in its ministry to troubled youth who come from disturbing pasts and harmful exposures, often with roots in a dysfunctional family history. Oakdale becomes a family of refuge and compassion, a social ecology of health, wholeness, and holy nurture. In the aggregate of faculty and staff, curriculum, physical setting, donor and prayer support, leadership, and student life, Oakdale is a special educational faith community, a wonderful Potter's wheel.

Colleges and Universities. A special Potter's wheel can be found in colleges and universities whose missions are Christ-centered and whose commitment is to the development of the whole student, head, heart, and life. This was my experience as a student at Asbury University. In the collective exposures to faculty, staff, and other students, the social/spiritual ecology of this school served as a Potter's wheel on which God shaped my heart and soul. It opened my eyes and ears to new ways of looking at the world. Those years were transformative, opening my heart to the inner workings of the Spirit. Originally, I wanted to go to a prestigious public university. I initially chose one. My father pushed me instead to a Wesleyan Holiness-oriented college. That paternal intervention was life-changing.

The school I attended was particularly powerful in its focus on integrating faith and learning in a holiness context. The possibility and privilege of holiness was clearly communicated in chapels, spiritual retreats, and personal conversations with particular professors and other spiritually mature student friends. In reflection now, I realize that the company I kept comprised the milieu that afforded an intense immersion in a kind of social/spiritual ecology. The process of my education included exposures that led to synergistic, sanctifying encounters with God.

I now interpret my formative college experience as immersions in social ecologies of holiness. More than occasional sprinklings of grace, the classes, chapels, meals together, genuine interest of faculty, and friendships with peers all comprised a social/spiritual milieu of holiness. The campus was a blend of academic excellence with piety and mercy. There I experienced a profound sense of God's holy, loving hands on my life through the influence of others shaping me in holiness and righteousness.

The idea of social ecologies of holiness describes settings of family life, life in the church, and in summer camps and college settings during those formative years. Along the way, the journey brought blessing in the exposures and encounters that shaped an awareness of and attentiveness to God's presence and love. As a result, my love for God and others matured. Various means of grace became habits-of-the-heart as the Holy Spirit guided my journey on a path of holiness and righteousness.

Those early formative experiences later served again to shape my appreciation for Christian higher education in the Wesleyan Holiness tradition, especially in another college where I served for several years, The Salvation Army's William and Catherine Booth University College in Winnipeg, Manitoba, Canada. The essence of Booth to this day is Jesus Christ. Christ's Spirit permeates the college to the extent that the Spirit permeates the hearts and lives of the faculty and staff. The desire is that the Spirit guide decisions about the curriculum, the content of studies, the goals of the academic programs, the spirit and manner in which higher education is delivered, and the social life characterizing an educational faith community. While Booth University College today aspires to academic excellence, it also strives to produce character, and by character it intentionally means character after the likeness of Jesus, to know him and in holiness to be like him. Competence in education and character in Spirit are its hallmarks.

Asbury University, Houghton College, Booth University College, and other holiness heritage colleges and universities are wheels of the divine Potter. Their undergraduate students learn on the Potter's wheel for four years. Where God is the Potter, a student's opportunity to pursue higher education has added value. It is "Higher" higher education. God's hand works through the sanctified company students keep with faculty, staff and each other. The entire metaphor speaks to the social-holiness nature of a Potter's wheel where the campus assists Christ in the spiritual formation of student lives.

Booth is not alone. Christian higher education in colleges and universities throughout North America and beyond can be a powerful means of grace, a kind of leaven in the bread of nations and cultures. Not all Christian colleges and universities succeed in this, but many do. They intentionally integrate holiness into all of campus life and remain devoted to student outcomes of holiness.[40] They are Potter's wheels, transformational ecologies of social holiness.

DISCUSSION QUESTIONS

1. Small behavior settings can be a Potter's wheel. What are the most effective Potter's wheels that God has used to shape your life?

2. Would you say that God is presently shaping the clay of your life in holiness, in your likeness to Jesus?

3. Is God's work in your life beautiful, functional, both?

4. How would you describe your present spiritual journey in light of John Wesley's ideas about higher and lower paths?

5. How have you helped Jesus shape the lives of others as his Potter's wheel?

ten

SPIRITUAL FORMATION: BEING PERFECTED

Be perfect, therefore, as your heavenly Father is perfect.
Matthew 5:48

When people come to faith in Christ and are active in the life of the church, each may be shaped into a particular kind of Christian in thought, word, and deed and still not be on a path to holiness. We saw this earlier in the Barna study (chapter two). They may have the habits and exposures of maturity, but not be growing in grace and Christ-likeness. While there's a commitment to the work of the church following initial salvation, the pure love of God and humble love of others may nevertheless remain lacking. The Christian life is more form than essence.

John Wesley had something to say about this. In 1787 he wrote a sermon entitled "The More Excellent Way." By this time in his life he had moved away from his earlier exclusivist standards of true faith and salvation. Perhaps initially he was influenced by an early church father, Clement of Alexandria, who proposed "two orders of Christians, each with its legitimate hope of salvation."

Wesley spoke of lower-road Christians who simply avoids doing evil, does good, attends the ordinances of God, and are not headed for hell. He then contrasted lower-road with higher-road Christians who seek the mind and heart of Christ and walk as he walked, suggesting that as a result they would have a higher place in heaven.

This sermon was written to encourage "lower order" believers to become more earnest Christians, to pursue "a more excellent way," essentially what George Barna in his ten transformational steps calls steps nine and ten, a profound love of God and a profound love of others. Such a pursuit progresses along the way of a full salvation. It's driven by a desire to be holy as God is holy (1 Peter 1:16), for without holiness no one will see the Lord (Hebrews 12:14).

This raises a question about whether social holiness is found in the idea that spiritual formation takes two forms, one with a lower degree of the presence and essence of God and the other that leads to a higher measure of God's grace and infilling essence. The one is a lower-order Christian, sincere and established in one form of the Christian life, yet struggling with holy discontent and prone to indifference to sin.

The other form of Christianity is spiritually shaped in the Christ-like life of the higher-order Christian, the believer who progresses through holy discontent and rises to complete surrender and submission to the will of God toward sanctification. The spiritual formation of the higher-order Christian is a progressive, balanced shaping of the head, heart, and life, especially the heart. The Apostle Paul called this a circumcision of the heart by the Spirit (Romans 2:29).

As Wesley matured in his own spiritual journey and reflections, his writings and sermons became more nuanced. He saw that, increasingly in obedient faith, higher-order Christians experience a process of sanctification. They grow in grace, dwell in Christ, and are shaped, strengthened, and established increasingly. Along the way of salvation they grasp the magnitude of the love of God with an expanding knowledge that surpasses knowledge, the knowledge of experience. They profoundly increase in their love for God in response to God's love. As they do, God grows their higher capacity to be entirely filled with and cleansed by the Holy Spirit (Ephesians 3:16-19).

In short, Wesley moved from a dualism of two levels, two paths, two roads of the Christian journey, to a continuum of grace, a journey with exposures and encounters. Along the way, in a dynamic, interactive, relational process of salvation, we experience what Kenneth Collins calls "synergistic sanctification."[41] We progress by grace through faith in Christ-likeness, encountering God in entire sanctification, followed by even more grace.

The lower-path Christian becomes seen as one in an early stage of spiritual formation, largely cognitive, gaining an appreciation of God's presence and identity but mostly in the form of doctrines and propositions. It's the state of knowing God, but not so much with a knowledge of the heart, the knowledge that surpasses knowledge (Ephesians 3:18). It's knowing mostly with the head. Moreover, one's experience of salvation is static, referencing past salvation from sin but not addressing continual sinning, and not going on to being perfected by God in increasing likeness to Christ.

Psalm 86:11 reads, "Teach me your way, LORD, that I may rely on your faithfulness; give me an undivided heart, that I may fear your name." Psalm 51:10 pleads, "Create in me a pure heart, O God, and renew a steadfast spirit within me." In making disciples, spiritual formation must engage more than the head and intellectual assents. It must be pursued through forms of learning that engage head, heart, and life together: knowing Christ, loving Christ, and living Christ. The spiritual formation of a disciple takes shape by the three spheres of intimacy that are increasingly growing together. These spheres increasingly overlap through God's perfecting grace, resulting in a growing intimacy and likeness to Jesus, the higher-order Christian.

High Paths are Lowly Paths

The paradox of the way of full salvation is that the higher path is a lowly path that challenges us with the toughest choices. Such lowly paths "require us to make sacrifices for good and not gain." The higher but lowly paths "call forth from us the courage to let go of the lesser ambitions of self-advancement for the greater ambitions of God's kingdom of grace, generosity, and compassion. They invite us to become big enough to become small, whatever our place in the social strata. There we will find the treasure, the meaning of our humanity, there the real fullness of life."[42]

In today's West, a great many people identify as Christians but are only culturally so. Millions are what Wesley called "almost Christians." They have never experienced repentance over past sins and sought forgiveness, redemption, and reconciliation with Christ. Furthermore, many true Christians are nonetheless in a static state of salvation. They have come to a stop. There is no progress, growth, forward movement. Their spiritual odometer shows little mileage and their spiritual formation is limited. They are minimalists, saved from past sin, yet sadly still sinning and not aspiring to holiness.

Those who have started but stopped are early-stage Christians, not that different in their daily lives, habits, and priorities from most people who are not followers of Jesus Christ at all. They are comfortable in the prevailing culture and remain babes in Christ, some for decades and maybe all of their lives. In contrast, there are relatively few higher-stage followers of Christ. The process of their formation is dynamic, moving forward, progressing in sanctifying grace, and moving on to glorifying grace. They are in the process of being completed in Christ Jesus. They are not perfect, but in their spiritual formation they are being perfected (1 John 2:5; 4:11-12).

Being Perfected

A greater degree of progress in spiritual formation never happens in a vacuum. It's necessarily occasioned by a healthy ecology in the presence of God, attentive to God's grace and the company of others. The lives and love of those others are God's means of shaping our lives, while our lives contribute to the godly shaping of others. God uses the company we keep and the company we provide as means of grace along the way toward holiness. We are being perfected with the help and support of others living in company with God, staying close to His heart (Jeremiah 13:1-11), continuing on the way of a full salvation.

We might use a sports illustration. I am an alumnus of Asbury University and the University of Kentucky. I became an avid fan of UK Wildcat basketball. The basketball metaphor makes sense to me when thinking about the power of social ecologies. The coach is very good at shaping the skills, savvy, and character of players. The coach's desire for his student players is that they excel as elite athletes and persons of character and be transformed into the best possible version of their preferred selves.

How is this excellence achieved? From the start, day after day, practice after practice, game after game, the student athletes are immersed in the company of the coach and coaching staff. They are continually being perfected into a higher capacity of play, and for some of the players to a successful career at the professional level. This is because the coaches and university provide a platform for the pursuit of perfection.

As the University of Kentucky basketball program is a high path for one day playing in the pros, socially spiritual ecologies of holiness are the platforms for spiritual formation of a higher order. They are the Potter's wheel. They prepare high-path Christians for a more excellent way and engage them in God's grace at a high level. By so doing they promote environments for sanctification and full salvation characterized by a profound loving of God and a profound loving of others.

What is meant by the phrase "being perfected" and what is the role of others in the pursuit of this perfection? Being perfected may sound lofty and elitist. It's true that no one is perfect in intellect and memory, in physical prowess and skills, and in the social graces in all circumstances. We never will be. We are limited especially in the spiritual domain. We are short on faith, obedience, and character. We are prone to wander, quick to sin, and short on humility, patience, and grace, even after repentance and faith in Christ as Lord and Savior.

Justification by faith does not mean we never sin again. We are innately vulnerable to temptation and prone to sin. Proverbs 24:16 says, "though the righteous fall seven times, they rise again, but the wicked stumble when calamity strikes." So, being "saved" does not mean perfection. There is no one who does not sin (1 Kings 8:46, Ecclesiastes 7:20, Romans 3:20). Nevertheless, where sin reigns God's grace can reign even more. We need not go on sinning. In Christ, by his grace, we need not live in sin any longer.

By faith we can come to live a new life (Romans 5:22-6:4). In short, as disciples living in faithful obedience, following Christ and obeying all that he commands (Matthew 28: 20), we can have power over sin. In my faith tradition, The Salvation Army, there is an article of faith that captures this possibility.[43] It is thoroughly Wesleyan and biblical and also includes a contingency. Continuance in a dynamic, relational, and progressive state of salvation depends on continuing faith in and obedience to Christ.

Jesus put it this way. "When you're joined with me and I with you, the relation intimate and organic, the harvest is sure to be abundant" (John 15:5, *The Message*). Humankind's greatest problem is not sin. It's the shortfall of loving God that leads to disobedience and the love of other gods. It's the long, sad history reported throughout Scripture. Jesus said three times, "If you love me, you will obey my commands" (John 14:15, 21, 23).

In obedient faith we can witness to others as to what the Holy Spirit is doing in our lives. God is perfecting us, transforming us into the likeness of Christ. We continue to progress by sanctifying grace when we freely choose to obediently place ourselves on particular wheels of the Potter. In social/spiritual contexts where God's grace is abundant, we are shaped into divine likeness. It's not that we're perfect or that it's impossible to sin. At any time we may yield to temptation and sin. Nevertheless, God's command is to "be perfect." As we remain in Christ and dwell in him, and his Spirit remains and dwells in us, we can be perfect in our will to obey his commands. We can be perfect *in our intentions, in purity of heart.*

We can be nourished by God's grace and grow in strength to love God and neighbor. God gives us strength and power over sin so that we may continue by His grace to grow and be perfected in His likeness. Continuing in such a dynamic, interactive (not static, passive) state, we become an encouragement to others with whom we keep company. In this way, we continually give and receive God's sanctifying grace. This is how social holiness works. We keep company with Christ through his grace as he makes us aware of his presence. Often God does this through and among the company of others for whom Christ is doing the same. This is the social ecology of holiness. Glory to God!

DISCUSSION QUESTIONS

1. How would you describe your present spiritual journey in light of John Wesley's ideas about higher and lower paths?

2. When you think of the people whose company you keep, are they growing in grace and walking in holiness? Does it seem like they live life in ways that please God? In what ways do you think they are having an influence on you?

3. Would you say you are in a dynamic, interactive relationship with Jesus Christ, knowing him more and more over time?

4. In what ways are you "being perfected?"

eleven

THE ECOLOGY OF HOLINESS

You will be like a well-watered garden,
like a spring whose waters never fail.

Jeremiah 58:11

The idea of an ecology of holiness aligns itself with formal research in the ecology of human development, a long-established field of scientific inquiry. Human ecology concerns itself with the "progressive accommodation between growing human organisms and their immediate environments."[44]

We are social and moral beings created in the image of God. We journey in social environments, the company of others. In their company, others influence our growth and spiritual formation. Depending on the path they are on with or without Christ, their presence has consequences for us and others. Keeping their company is the context in which we remain either static and stagnant or strengthened in faith. The immediate social/spiritual environment of others may be salutary or toxic, spiritually healthy or poisonous, like prolonged exposure to low levels of radiation.

Let's go back to John Wesley's sermon "The More Excellent Way" and the idea of a high path or plane of holiness. Depending on the company we keep, we risk stasis and little or no spiritual progress. Ecologically speaking, the low plane is like a spiritual desert where the resources are minimally available or unavailable. If you've lived in or even just visited Arizona, you will immediately remember the difference between the heat in the desert environment of Phoenix and the pine trees and skiing opportunities of Flagstaff. The trip from Phoenix up to Flagstaff reminds me of the old chorus we used to sing:

> *Lord lift me up where I can stand*
> *By faith on heaven's table land.*
> *A higher plane than I have found,*
> *Lord plant my feet on higher ground.*

The high plane of sustained, obedient faith offers a very different ecology. The company of sanctified others brings about the presence of Christ and an abundance of resources in the fellowship of spiritually mature others. The path even through desert settings runs along streams and from oasis to oasis of fellowship and grace. Along the way, God's provision of grace is more than sufficient to support continual growth and fruitfulness.

A caveat is needed. The imagery of spiritual low and high paths or planes is compelling, but it's potentially misleading. It can be mistakenly understood and wrongly imply an elitism of the high-road over lower-road pilgrims. Such a divergence may be misperceived as a higher spiritual and a lower physical reality—a dualism. It may suggest too simplistically a bifurcation of the journey of faith into only two categories when in reality the journey is along a continuum of grace and progressive sanctification.

As we progress in holiness, we climb to a higher plane where the social/spiritual conditions of growth and sanctification are more abundant. We are social and moral beings created in the image of God. We journey in the company of others. Their lives influence a process of continuing growth and spiritual formation. Depending on the social/spiritual experience (positive or negative, healthy or toxic) of others along the way, their presence has consequences for all with whom they interact.

In the company of others, we remain to a degree either static and stagnant or strengthened and growing in faith. In this way, social holiness is ecological. It is occasioned by the company we keep and by the continuing dynamic, interactive presence and work of the Holy Spirit in our lives in and through the lives of others.

The Ecology of Grace

Holy Scripture is abundant in its use of spiritually ecological metaphors. A few examples:

Psalm 1:1-3. Blessed is the man who… is like a tree planted by streams of water, which yields its fruit in season and whose leaf does not wither; whatever he does prospers.

Colossians 2:6-7. So just as you received Christ as Lord, continue to live in him, rooted and built up in him, strengthened in the faith as you were taught.

Ephesians 3:17a, 19b. So that Christ may dwell in your hearts through faith. And I pray that you, being rooted and established in love… may be filled to the measure of the fullness of God.

John 15:1, 5, 8. I am the true vine, and my Father is the gardener.... If a man remains in me and I remain in him, he will bear much fruit.... This is to my Father's glory, that you bear much fruit, showing yourselves to be my disciples.

Isaiah 55:10-11. As the rain and the snow come down from heaven, and do not return to it without watering the earth and making it bud and flourish, so that it yields seed for the sower and bread for the eater, so is my word that goes out from my mouth; it will not return to me empty, but will accomplish what I desire and achieve the purpose for which I sent it.

2 Peter 3:18. Grow in grace and the knowledge of our Lord and Savior Jesus Christ.

The words associated with new life in Christ are organic and ecological: seeds, soil, growth, roots, vine, branches, leafs, trees, and fruit.

When Scripture speaks of the fruit of the Spirit, it references nine core characteristics of the Christian life. Together they comprise a description of the personhood of Christ. Visible growth provides a picture of holiness in the likeness of Christ. The seed is full of potential and promise. The seed's DNA is designed for maturity and fruitfulness. That potential is contingent on conditions of a healthy ecology. When all the elements and means are continually present, even the tiny mustard seed grows as God intends.

For the past two summers I've planted a small garden. The first year I tilled the ground and fertilized the soil. The result was rather pitiful. The next year I mixed several bags of manure into the soil. The results were a little better. The corn I planted looked a bit pathetic by mid-July, but good enough to be ravaged by hungry racoons. I obviously needed help in understanding the means of growing a robust garden. Meanwhile, I had dear friends who have been composting for years and building up a rich base of soil with all the right elements to promote optimal growth. Their gardens are amazing, bursting with results. By mid-July they are delivering bags of tomatoes, cucumbers, and summer squash to all their friends.

The gardens are distinct ecologies with different capacities for nurturing growth and fruitfulness. Initially, both had a degree of potential for productive results, but my garden lacked the nutrient-rich elements that enable expected results. The friend's garden had all the means to produce an abundance. The difference was in the means appropriate to the task: proper soil, sun, and the right amount of water.

Parable of the Sower. Mark 4:3-9. Jan Luyken.

When Peter says "grow in grace" (2 Peter 3:18) and uses the little word "in," he is talking about an ecology of grace and holiness. The "in" contextualizes holiness. Ecology is that branch of science that deals with the relationship between organisms and their environments. The key to thinking and speaking ecologically is to acknowledge that every living thing is immersed in a context or environment that has specific characteristics that determine outcomes.

Consider the ecology of a tadpole in a pristine pond, enriched by nutrients and free of toxins, an ideal environment for growth and reproduction. There is such a pond. It lies high in the White Mountains of New Hampshire. When my children and I were younger, we backpacked together and one afternoon came upon it. Fed by a cold mountain stream from the previous winter's snow, the pond was inviting. After hiking on that hot summer afternoon, we sought the pond's cool comfort. We took the plunge. It was an especially memorable moment. I still wonder to what degree we changed the nearly perfect ecology of that pond by our dusty, sweaty bodies.

Every living thing in that pond defines its ecology. It's the ecology of the pond that sustains the life of all the organisms in it. A little human sweat would not have much ecological impact, but a steady supply of industrial waste would turn the pond from pristine to toxic.

One summer I worked on a freighter on the Great Lakes. One evening our ship docked in Cleveland, about a half-mile up the Cuyahoga River. The river was a cesspool of industrial waste. Heavy industry along the river had for years belched the most disgusting and deadly substances into the water. So polluted was the river that when a seaman on another ship finished a cigarette and threw it into the water, the river actually caught fire. The fire grew. It became a blaze and floated toward Lake Erie, doing some damage along the way.

The story doesn't end as an ecological disaster. Toxic ecologies can be transformed and experience redemptive, restorative outcomes. In this case, through great community resolve, the river was dramatically cleaned up. Gone today are the industrial toxins.

A thriving economy of restaurants and tourist attractions now exist along the banks. The Cuyahoga River is a marvellous example of ecological restoration, creation care, a marvelous metaphor for transformation to holiness.

Years later I was working on a research project in South Korea with faculty at Seoul National University. My gracious Korean colleagues hosted me at a special restaurant in the countryside. The place was renowned in South Korea for its excellent variety of fish and the wonderful ways that chefs prepared them. The fish were raised in such a way as to maximize their flavor from the day they were selected and imported from Israel. By establishing a nutrient-enriched, well-aerated, temperature-controlled environment, the fish farmers grew a high quality, tasty fish for this restaurant.

Environments have consequences. When the Apostle Peter says, "Grow in the grace of the Lord," he is speaking ecologically. He implies our immersion into a nourishing, nutrient-healthy, wholesome ecology of holiness where we may grow by God's provision of all possible means of grace.

Ecological Means of Growth in Grace

What is it specifically about the company of others as means of grace that catalyzes and energizes the transforming work of the Holy Spirit? What is the specific nature of the means of grace to be found in ecologies of holiness? How do they work to change us into the likeness of Jesus?

Henry Knight's work offers a helpful framework of how John Wesley conceives of the means of grace in the Christian life and the transformation they occasion in our continuing salvation.[45] Wesley's understanding is grounded in appreciation of God's presence and identity. It's by faith that God's presence, identity, and character are perceived. Faith is a gift of God. It often is received in a social context where participants are encouraged and enabled by the help of others to see themselves and all of life before God.

Knight makes clear that the identity and presence of God can be known only by faith through participation in those means of grace that convey God's identity and draw us nearer to God and a fuller awareness of the divine presence. These include Scripture, prayer, thanksgiving, praise, confession, acts of mercy, fasting, sacraments, and the highly ecological practice of conference (community discussion).

Wesley makes particular mention of the general means of grace such as watching, practicing awareness of God's presence, doing no harm, avoiding evil, and exercising self-denial, a precondition for taking up one's cross. By all of these means we may do all the good we can. Although we do them freely, these practices are not so much acts of discipline as they are intentional responses to God's grace. General means of grace presuppose and strengthen faith.

In the company of others, we receive and pass on God's grace. The company we give and receive is a means of grace at the heart of social holiness. Small gatherings make possible the social support helpful to staying attentive to the presence of God and the likelihood of recognizing God's character and grace. The means of grace received and experienced in our relationships with others help maintain an active relationship with God.

Moreover, we become more like Jesus when we in love pass grace on to others. This is the dynamic life we have in Christ and in Christian community. Outside of such community, we become attentive to and distracted by the things of the world. When we become insensitive to the presence and grace of God, faith dissipates. As faith dissipates, so does our likeness to Christ.

Means of grace inform us of and make real to us God's presence, identity, and character. They open our hearts to God's love and occasion the outpouring of love to others. They are how we encounter and respond to the living God in obedient faith to His command to love God with all our strength, soul, mind and heart, and to love our neighbour as ourselves. The God we seek is the God who readily reveals Himself through these means and anticipates our receptivity, recognition, and continuing response.

This interactive social process presupposes a devoted Christian community (Acts 2:42-47) wherein each person is mutually supported and held accountable to God and others. This was the nature of Wesley's small groups (class meetings and bands). They were *ecclesiolae* (little churches) in *ecclesia* (big church), each one a socially spiritual ecology leading to holiness.

Ecologies of Holiness

The discussion throughout this book is about the orthodoxy of social holiness in the context of Wesleyan thought. John Wesley was skilled at articulating the Christian *orthodoxy* of a full salvation, but equally skilled in the spread of a biblical holiness through an accompanying *orthopraxy*. This took the form of small group gatherings called class meetings and bands, a defining characteristic of Wesley's Methodist movement. We recognize them as organic ecologies of holiness.

Wesley's ecologies of holiness provided the opportunity for spiritual accountability. On our own, we tend to make decisions and wander into social and spiritual contexts that are toxic. As the hymn goes, we are "prone to wander." As a dynamic ecological metaphor, accountability to others is a kind of prophylactic that works against temptation. It's a spiritual anti-oxidant against the cancer of sin. Wesley's "bands" occasioned a higher level of spiritual maturity and sanctified life.

The praxis of small accountability groups included a "penitent" group of people who failed to participate in the life of their group with transparency and confidentiality. If they wished to remain in the overall Methodist society, they had to endure active membership in a remedial group of other struggling penitents. All of Wesley's small groups were arrayed along the continuum of God's grace from prevenient, to justifying, sanctifying, and glorifying grace. In this way, the orthopraxy of his accountability groups was an expression of his theological orthodoxy. Holiness of heart and life and glory to God were the goal all the way along.

Holiness on Its Way

The Gospel of Christ, as it comes to us from others, should be on its way to someone else. So it is with holiness. It comes to us through many means of grace, but especially through the social, relational presence and engagement of others in the form of small groups. In Jesus' own words, "Where two or three gather in my name, there I am with them" (Matthew 19:20).

The full gospel is the story of God's love embodied in a full salvation from the uttermost of disobedience and sin to the uttermost of holiness, growth in grace, sanctification, the fullness of God, and purity of heart and life. It's a story of God's grace in light of our disobedience. It's boundless love and favor drawing us. It's God's desire to restore us individually and as a people to holiness. God uses the company of others who also are being perfected to carry out His desire for them and us.

The church is God's universal community of saints. Communities of saints ideally comprise ecologies of holiness that function as channels of divine power and potential to establish others in the Kingdom of God. In the company (social context) of saints, holiness comes to us on its way to someone else and, as saints in the making, we are privileged to participate in the divine nature that makes that possible. This is consistent with the idea that "we become the company we keep."

The gospel is God's story. It runs from Genesis through the Bible to the last page of the Book of Revelation. It's the narrative of God's redemptive, reconciling, work of our salvation and restoration from inevitable death to the certainty of everlasting life and the redemption of creation. It's the good news of salvation that comes to us as "the continuing work of Jesus by the Holy Spirit, through the church, to the world."[46] The gospel came to us through the church, through others and, depending on our faithfulness as God's agents, forward to someone else.

It's been that way since Jesus began preaching "Repent for the kingdom of heaven is at hand" (Matthew 4:17). The kingdom is here now, yet still coming. As it came to us, it is still going on to others. The message of a full salvation comes to others by the Spirit through others. By the grace of God, the gospel was passed on to us through the company we've kept with other Christians. Our faithfulness in sharing the full story of salvation with others is our way of responding to God's holy love for us. God lavishes grace on us and waits for our obedient response to make disciples and "grow saints."

Life is not meant to be lived alone and yet so many people are alone. They live socially and spiritually marginalized, on the periphery of the good news of the gospel, unloved and unaware of God's grace. They are the homeless on the streets and hiding in the green spaces of urban settings. They are on mass transit and caught in traffic, sitting in public parks, local taverns, coffeeshops, or fast food establishments, corporate cubicles, and company cafeterias.

So many hearts yearn for contact and love from someone, yet they keep the company of no one. Contacts that do come are superficial, shallow, and bureaucratic at best. They miss out on the love of Christ because of our inattentiveness to God's voice. In the words of vocal artist Steve Green, "People need the Lord." They need God's company. The last verse of the song says it well:

People need the Lord, people need the Lord.
At the end of broken dreams, He's the open door.
People need the Lord, people need the Lord.
When will we realize that we must give our lives,
For people need the Lord.

The gospel came to us through someone, usually through several others over time. It's to be shared with others.

The seed of the Word best flourishes to the glory of God in the context of ecologies of holiness when and where high-plane, Spirit-filled Christians come together for the work of bringing God's prevenient, justifying, sanctifying, and glorifying grace to a desperately broken world. As God's grace is brought, it comes to others as it came to us, in open, inviting hospitality and love. The invitation is so inclusive that we become the company others really do keep and together with them we are being perfected in the context of that hospitality.

Holiness is being filled to the measure of the fullness of God. It's not impossible nor out of reach. It's not for the spiritually elite nor something to strive for and personally achieve. It's for all. It's free and full. Like our initial salvation, it's a gift from God by faith. It's not something that is merely personal, but to be shared, deployed, and engaged as we participate in God's transformation and restoration of creation. Our love for God and others is to be so sanctified and profound that our subsequent life's service ultimately brings glory to God.

DISCUSSION QUESTIONS

1. In thinking about your spiritual development in social/spiritual settings, is your situation like a construction site where you are being built-up and established or a garden where you are rooted and growing?

2. What is the nature of the ecclesiolae in your life?

3. Where would you place yourself along Wesley's salvation path of prevenient, justifying, sanctifying, and glorifying grace?

4. If one's life in the Spirit is ecological in nature, what are the nutrients in your spiritual ecology that promote healthy spirituality and a sustained life of holiness?

5. What Scripture passages help you appreciate the idea of an ecology of holiness?

twelve

TELOS

Aim at... a holy life.

Hebrews 12:14

T*elos* is a word in Greek that means something toward which we aim. It's a goal, end, or purpose. The word applies to the idea of salvation. The *telos* of salvation may differ depending on the teaching of a particular religion. Within Christian belief, even within evangelical understanding, the telos of salvation can differ, with accompanying consequences for understanding holiness and holy living.

Missing the Mark

I introduced the idea of "bus stop religion" in chapter two. It's the unfortunate idea that the *telos* of salvation is basically, even only, avoiding hell and getting to heaven. It assumes that once we confess our sins, repent, and accept Jesus' sacrifice for us on the cross, that's it. We've been handed our heavenly ticket. That's all there is to it other than waiting for departure.

We've achieved the purpose of God's sacrificial provision of salvation.

As the full aim of salvation, however, this misses the mark. The bigger picture is not personal self-interest for the purpose of heaven-bound transit and divine fire insurance. Rather than *transportation*, the core idea is *transformation*.

God's *telos* for us is our transformation. It's reconciliation of our relationship with God for the purpose of our restoration and the healing of all creation. Salvation is redemption from penalty or punishment for disobedience and sin. It's made possible by Christ's sacrifice on the cross and his resurrection to eternal life. But there is more. It's also power over sin provided by the indwelling presence of the Holy Spirit. It's the privilege of participating in God's personhood and nature. Our being is to be infused with the essence of God, which in turn makes possible perfect love for God and others.

Salvation is the privilege of partnering with God in His great project of restoration. That participation includes loving our neighbor with God's perfect, holy love that transforms us and others. Accompanied by sanctified others and God's presence in us, we become a redemptive and restorative presence. In our transformation together, we become agents of God's restorative, transformative love to the world. That's a life of missional importance. That's social holiness.

The privilege of our sanctification came to us through obedient others who were instrumental in sharing the gospel of a full salvation with us. God used the faithful presence, witness, and engagement of others to position us by grace through faith for our redemption, reconciliation, and radical transformation. God continues to grow, shape, and transform us in holiness, not only to bless us personally, but to use us in service and witness in order to transform, heal, make whole, sanctify, and fill others with God's Spirit.

Holiness is not the ultimate end, however. Our personal holiness is part of God's vision of the ultimate *telos*. Every individual, family, workplace, faith community, local community, and nation that shows the marks of belonging and contributing to an ecology of holiness participates in the Kingdom of God and the healing of all creation. Anything less is missing the mark.

Two Ecologies in Tension

Every young person raised in an ecology of full salvation learned that God is the Creator, Preserver, and Governor of all things. God's initial glory is in his creation. When I think of that truth, I remember John Muir. He was one of my childhood heroes.

Muir (1838-1914) was a Scottish-American naturalist, author, and environmental philosopher. When it came to valuing creation, he had his boots on the ground and that made him an early advocate for the preservation of the wilderness throughout the United States. He was a passionate campaigner for preserving thousands of acres of what are now our national parks.

In his day, Muir was the prime mover for preserving creation and the eventual establishment of the U. S. National Park system. His legacy is our blessing. So much of God's creation is now preserved for posterity's appreciation. If you've ever been to Yosemite, the Grand Canyon, Niagara Falls, or any of the other national parks, you realize that God's glorious works remain beyond our limited imagination, but through them we appreciate nature's remarkable diversity and beauty and God's unparalleled creativity. Muir was God's agent on behalf of our ability to appreciate.

Yet, who can doubt that all of creation is now under siege, decimated, and suffering on-going ecological destruction. Forests and whole species are being depleted or even completely disappearing. Extreme climate disasters are more frequent. Ecological devastation and famine occasion human poverty and migration.

Climatologists and oceanographers concur in their respective fields of research and expertise: the earth's temperature is rising. The earth is running a fever. The oceans are warming and rising.

Largely as a result of human influence, the earth is close to irreversibly crossing ecological thresholds from which there is no turning back. In all of this, the phrase "human influence" turns out to be a euphemism for sin. In Genesis 2:15-18 we read that God made humankind, put them in a garden to work and take care of it. Since then, the directive hasn't changed. What has changed and remains today is the consequence of humankind's disobedience, dereliction of duty, and continuing sin.[47]

The toxic ecologies throughout creation are not independent of the toxicity of the social/spiritual ecologies created by humanity's disobedience and sin. If we can imagine a *telos* of holiness, God's desire for all humankind in which we are being restored and perfected in Christ Jesus by the Spirit, can we imagine the devastation of the opposite?

Consider the reality of ecologies of sin, of "human influence" that marginalizes, discriminates against, dishonors, disparages, degrades, desecrates, and destroys. Notice the progression: first marginalizes, discriminates, and dishonors, then disparages and degrades the inherent value of something, and then destroys altogether. Sin desecrates and destroys. To desecrate is to violate the sacredness of something. Sin does this in all areas of God's creation.

As holiness is ecological, so is sin. Instead of being characterized by the health, wholeness, and holiness benefits of God's pure, holy love, the ecology of sin is just the opposite. Its nature is toxic and poisonous. Its *telos* follows a path of desecration, decay, and destruction. It thrives on the loneliness, vulnerability, and misery of alienation. When we are in an ecology of sin, we are not in a vacuum. We are in an alternative ecological, spiritual context, vulnerable and self-alienated from the presence of God.

Ecologies of sin are integrative and inclusive of all areas of creation. They exist in stark contrast to the ecologies of holiness as darkness is to light. We are reminded that the Gospel of John opens with this about Jesus: "In him was life, and that life was the light of men" (John 1:4). Jesus said, "I am the light of the world" (John 8:12) and "Let your light shine in such a way that others see your good works and glorify the Father" (Matthew 5:16).

Howard Snyder points out that the ecology of sin is alienation along four dimensions: from God; from each other; from ourselves; and from the global environment.[48] He crafts an understanding of salvation in two contexts: the ecology of sin and the ecology of saving grace. The ecology of sin "cries out for an ecology of salvation." Snyder says that sin exists as disobedience to God and brings alienation. Alienation is estrangement and complete separation from God due to sin. It's a key focus of the biblical narrative.

The sad story goes on. Sin is a malady, a disease that infects humanity and is passed down from generation to generation. As an infection, sin permeates and affects all areas and dimensions of life. As a disease, sin must be healed. We are born into sin and estranged from our Creator, the source of all life, well-being, health, and hope. When we sin, we self-alienate from God, from self, others, and from the land.

As Snyder explains, the *telos* is salvation from sin and the creation healed. Social holiness should be understood as the process of restoring our love relationship as individuals and as people with God and all creation. Social holiness pursues restoration through God's means of the perfect love of others, of self, and of all aspects of the world. It's an expression of a synergistic and symbiotic relationship of God, humankind, and creation.

With the help of Snyder's perspective, we may consider an enlarged definition of full salvation. The antidote to the ecology of sin is the ecology of holiness. The love of Christ clearly compels us to seek out, promote, and establish ecologies of holiness for ourselves and others in response to a world that is rife with ecologies of sin, degradation, and destruction. It's now possible to pursue our participation in the drama of God's full salvation. The *telos* is the healing of all creation.

Social Holiness in Community

> I thank you Lord that when I pray I do not pray alone, but with the deep help of your Spirit and in the company of saints and martyrs. Lord, I join my prayers and cries and intercessions with your faithful, godly people: May your kingdom come! May your will be done on earth as in heaven until the earth is "full of the knowledge of the Lord as the waters cover the sea" (Isaiah 11:9). Amen.
>
> Howard Snyder

Social holiness is the dynamic, interpersonal expression of Christian community, the biblical holiness of God's family. As Snyder explains: "It is the active work and witness of God's community of earth and heaven: (1) by Christ through the Holy Spirit (John 1:3); (2) locally with one another (1 John 1:7); (3) with the broader Church within one's region or nation (Acts 1:8 and 20:1-4); (4) with the Global church, 'All Christian sisters and brothers throughout the earth' (Ephesians 2:19); (5) with 'all people of God in all times and places, in heaven and earth, by the Spirit and in the Trinity' (Hebrews 11:1-12); and (6) in 'solidarity with the entire human family on earth and with all creation' (Ephesians 3:14)."

Personal holiness remains the historically desired *telos* of individuals in the cultural context of individualism in the West. A purpose of this book, however, is to broaden our understanding of the social nature of holiness. It underscores the social/spiritual origins of holiness in Christ by the Spirit and the ultimate purpose of social holiness. It's more than becoming one's personal best. It's more than gaining a personal blessing for ourselves, our circle of friends, and those whose company we keep. The aim also includes salvation as healing our physical world. While it's the privilege of all believers to be wholly sanctified on the personal path of salvation, social holiness includes all creation's healing.

The Ultimate *Telos*

The overarching purpose or *telos* of salvation is even more than creation healed. It will be the glorious and boundless joy of perfect love and life as the whole of the human family over time and place will be united in a new creation in the everlasting presence of God. That will be the Kingdom of God now and yet to come, the ultimate *telos*!

There is a simple phrase that captures the ultimate *telos* of holiness and creation healed. It is "Glory to God!" Glory to God is the aim of personal holiness, of social holiness, and the reason for making disciples and teaching them to obey everything that Jesus commands. "Glory to God" is the purpose of redemption, reconciliation, and restoration to the likeness of Christ. It's the purpose of sanctifying grace, of being perfected, transformed, and becoming a new creation as a people. It's the *telos* of the creation healed, the Kingdom of God now and the new creation yet to come. The purpose of a new heaven and a new earth is glory to God!

The Bible encourages thanks, praise, and glory to God. God's grace is lavished on us again and again. When God's grace is recognized and acknowledged, humanity's response to God's boundless salvation and deep ocean of love is to give Him glory. Giving glory to God in obedient faith is how we show love to God in return. Paul writes to the church at Galatia, "The only thing that counts is faith expressing itself in love" (Galatians 5:6). John writes, "We love God because he first loved us" (1 John 1:14). Glory to God!

In the intimate dynamic of God's profound love for us, and our profound love for God and others, such love compels us to higher heights of service. Paul captures the immensity of God's love and its transformative power for service in his sharing with the church at Ephesus (Ephesians 3:14-21) and makes clear what makes such heights possible. This remarkable passage contains all the transition points of Wesley's *via salutis*.

Paul is writing to established Christians in Ephesus who have come to faith in Christ. He starts by introducing the social/spiritual context of his message. It derives from his own intimate time with God in prayer. Paul is a mature Christian for whom prayer is not only praise, thanks, and petition, but also listening. In the listening, the Holy Spirit had had shared with him what he was to write to the Ephesians and to us. He prays that God may strengthen them and us with power and do so in their (our) inner beings by Christ taking up residence and indwelling.

God has the resources to answer Paul's prayer and is able to infuse the Ephesians and us with divine power that only the Holy Spirit can provide. God's power does not manifest itself in outward physical prowess so much as in inner strength of character open to the continuing presence of Christ in the heart. Paul thinks of the Ephesians as mature, rooted and established in love. This is a familiar echo of Paul: "Just as you received Christ Jesus as Lord, continue to live in him, rooted and built up in him, strengthened in the faith" (Colossians 2:7).

Paul goes on writing to the Ephesians with a stress on social holiness. Assuming their grounding in love, he prays that they may have power not on their own, but with all the saints. He reminds them that, as Christ Jesus dwells in them and they continue in Christ, Christ brings with him all the saints. The totality of Christ's continual presence, and of all the saints who accompany him, comes with faith and makes up God's extensive ecology of holiness.

Paul then goes on to explain what the power is that God provides. It's the power to grasp the magnitude of God's love. Paul's concern is not that these believers get a glimpse of God's love, or touch it with a wisp of reflection from time to time. Rather, he uses the word "grasp." They and we should get an iron grip on a profound reality. To grasp the truth of what God wants to share is not merely an exercise in some intellectual agreement with a theological proposition, to know cognitively about love. His prayer is that they know God's love with a knowledge that surpasses knowledge, that they know it profoundly with their hearts.

How else can the love of God be truly known? It's not a matter of the mind alone. Paul is talking about God's love, a matter of the heart. The scope of Paul's prayer reminds us of the Sunday school song, "Wide, wide as the ocean, high as the heaven above, deep, deep as the deepest sea, is my Savior's love." It highlights William Booth's "O Boundless Salvation, Deep Ocean of Love." Paul prays that we who believe should grasp with head and heart "how wide and long and high and deep is the love of Christ." If we can do that, we will be ready for the even greater grace that follows.

The Greater Grace

Paul makes clear that the *telos* of our faith is found in the context of Christ's intimacy, in his dwelling in our hearts, by our faithful continuance in Christ in the company of all the saints. God's amazing *telos* for us is revealed when Paul writes "that you may be filled to the measure of the fullness of God." It's holiness, the sanctified infilling of God, and the gift of a pure heart. Paul's prayers paint a portrait of holiness that reminds us of his expression, "Christ in you, the hope of glory" (Colossians 1:27).

As remarkable as the Ephesians 3:16-19 passage sounds, God's *telos* of holiness in us is not the ultimate *telos*, nor even is the salvation of creation healed. The ultimate *telos* is found in the turn Paul finally takes. He steps off of the phrase "filled to the measure of the fullness of God" into a proclamation that is the ultimate *telos*. He does so with one little but gigantic word. "Now."

Now what? Now we are filled to the measure of the fullness of God, GLORY! Holiness is socially experienced in the presence of God and others. It is experienced by faith expressing itself in love. It's a personal *telos* toward a greater *telos* in which "salvation is creation healed." NOW, in the light of an empowered life of service compelled by a profound love of God and others, incredible service surpassing belief, we find ourselves on the receiving end of an even greater grace of the God who can do immeasurably more than we could ask or imagine.

Now, in holiness, God is able to do immeasurably more in us, through us, and among us toward Kingdom ends. Now, in holiness, we are able to love, serve, and worship God like never before and in ways and to degrees that are beyond anything we could ask for or imagine, with all bringing Glory to God! "Now... glory to God!" Scripture makes it clear (Ephesians 3:21). The ultimate *telos*, the aim of all life in Jesus Christ and through him the power to love profoundly, the purpose of our creation, of all creation, and of creation healed and new, is glory to God!

Together with All the Saints

The greater grace of God is a shared grace with all the saints. It's easy to revert to our culturally-driven ways of thinking about Paul's message to the Ephesians, as if he is speaking only to the individual. Our inclination is to think only in a private and individual manner and consider glory to God as the substance of one's personal fidelity and testimony. Paul's prayers are about life in the social ecology of community, "together with all the saints."

The collective ecology of faith is Paul's focus, so much so that his letter is not only to the Ephesians. It's a circular letter. The church at Ephesus is the hub of the wheel, the *ecclesia* of the region from which the letter is circulated to the *ecclesiolae* of the churches in the surrounding smaller towns and villages. It's addressed and spoken to the "y'all" of the gathered saints so that the ecologies of the emerging counter-culture will be one collective ecology of faith expressing itself in love to the glory of God.

The ultimate *telos* is the together with all the saints, the church, the community in mission.[49] Our faith journey becomes the leaven in the bread of the existing, toxic culture. When the holiness is social, it becomes a collective testimony to the glory of God. Now, together, it's possible to make disciples and grow saints like never before. Glory to God!

DISCUSSION QUESTIONS

1. If a *telos* is something toward which you aim, what presently is your spiritual *telos*?

2. What persons in your life help you define your *telos* and succeed in realizing it?

3. If the ultimate personal *telos* is holiness, fullness of God's holy love, the indwelling of the Holy Spirit, and purity of heart, with whom do you share the same *telos*?

4. What does it mean for you and the company you keep to fulfill Christ's directive to "let your light shine so that others see your good work and glorify God the Father"?

5. In what ways does your life, and the lives of the company you keep, reflect the ultimate *telos* of the Christian life, glory to God?

thirteen

REACHING OUT: ALL GLORY TO GOD

*Very truly I tell you, whoever believes in me will
do the works I have been doing, and they will
do even greater things than these...*

John 14:12

*Let your light shine before others,
that they may see your good deeds
and glorify your father in heaven...*

Matthew 5:16

Early in Jesus' ministry He said to His disciples that a day would come that they and others would do greater things than what they had witnessed in His ministry. He said that whatever they asked in His name in the future, He would do "so that the Father may be glorified in the Son." The context for saying this was just before Jesus reached out for a bowl of water and a towel to wash the feet of His disciples, an exemplary act of servitude (John 13:2-17, 34).

Jesus went on to say: "A new command I give you. Love one another. As I have loved you, love one another." The message in the moment was that their Lord had given them an example of servant-like relationship and ministry, self-giving love that brings awe and glory to God.

With the infilling of the Holy Spirit comes the power to love as God loves. God's love is most clearly seen in Jesus who was and is full of grace and truth. We see God's glory in Jesus humbly washing the feet of each disciple prior to their last meal together. With the bowl of water and towel, His taking on the work of a servant was the prelude to His greatest glory, the cross. His sacrificial love for the world made possible the remission of our sins and the amazing grace that enables our salvation.

There is no greater glory than that described by the Apostle Paul regarding God's love in Christ Jesus "who, being in very nature God… made himself nothing by taking the very nature of a servant, being made in human likeness… he humbled himself by becoming obedient to death—even the death of the cross" (Philippians 2:6-8).

The idea of glory to God (Ephesians 3:20-21) is not the common idea of glory that we find in the self-oriented, self-serving, self-glorifying culture of self-pride. Self-adulation and personal esteem celebrate individual achievements and great personal accomplishments. On a social level, getting glory is the pursuit of striving to elevate one's self. It's the identification with and adoration of athletes and teams, cinema and media stars, and otherwise famous persons. Instead, glory to God aligns us with the humility, service, self-denial, and sacrificial love we see in Jesus at His most glorious moment on the cross. His glory is defined by that self-giving moment of God's pure, holy love reaching out for our sake, for our benefit, for the salvation of the world.

The "glory to God" is found in the fullness of God's love reaching out to others in social holiness through the Body of Christ. It's the social holiness of all the saints who together grasp the magnitude of God's love in humility, self-denial, and self-sacrificing service to others. Such service brings glory to God. God's love-compelled service can only come from a divine infilling, and it's only by God's love that we together can do "immeasurably more than we ask or imagine." It's not we who are able to do great things, but God at work in us.

Reaching Out

Reaching out to others as God's people with the self-giving, holy love of God is a long and continuing narrative down through history. Since Pentecost, God in His Trinitarian fullness has showered the gathered saints with the Holy Spirit, making it possible for them to reach out in Spirit-enabled love, service and sacrifice. Filled with the Spirit as God's means of grace, saints together are empowered by God to do immeasurably more than they or we could imagine, all to the glory of God. Here are some highlights and examples.

The Early Church (Acts 2:44-47). Scripture makes it clear. "All the believers were *together* and had everything in common. They sold property and possessions to give to anyone who had need. Every day they continued to meet together in the temple courts. They broke bread in their homes and ate together with glad and sincere hearts." The nascent church, a new community of faith, was a growing fellowship of saints. In their life together there was a collective sensitivity to the needs of others. In love for one another, they relationally reached out in acts of love and mercy. It's no wonder that "the Lord added to their number daily those who were being saved" (Acts 2:47).

The Church in Antioch (Acts 11:27-30). During the time when Barnabas and Paul were teaching the multi-cultural, multi-ethnic community of faith at Antioch, "some prophets came down from Jerusalem to Antioch. One of them named Agabus stood up and through the Spirit predicted that a severe famine would spread over the entire Roman world." The disciples there in Antioch, as each was able, decided together to provide help for the believers living in Judea. This they did by sending their gift to the elders by Barnabas and Saul. The social holiness of affective and material solidarity between the Body of Christ at Antioch and their brothers and sisters in Christ in Jerusalem was not an isolated event, not one and done. It was now to be the way of life in Christ.

We see elsewhere the same expression of caring and sharing reflecting the unity of the church broadly (Romans 15:26-27, 1 Corinthians 16:1-4). We see also in Galatians 2:10 a remembering of the poor, something the Apostle Paul was eager to see disciples do all along. These practical acts of love, reaching out to others, is reminiscent of John Wesley's favorite verse which sums up the virtue of reaching out: "The only thing that counts is faith expressing itself in love" (Galatians 5:6b).[50] In short, "the essence of social holiness is seen in holy love with others reaching out to others."[51]

The Ancient Church (100-400 AD). In the writings of the early church fathers, Cyprian of Carthage, Tertullian, Clement of Alexandria, Justin Martyr, Perpetua, and Dyonisius all write graphic descriptions of the remarkable faith expressed in love for one another in the church. The preeminent social model that defined the Christian church was the strong-group Mediterranean family. "God was the Father of the community, Christians were brothers and sisters. Over the aspirations and desires of the individual, the group came first. Family values—ranging from intense emotional attachment and the sharing of material goods to uncompromising family loyalty—determined the relational ethos of Christian behavior."[52] This picture of the early church is one of social holiness within the family of God, a remarkable, counter-cultural, self-sacrificing love for one another.

Medieval Settings (about 500 to 1500). In the early Middle Ages, the vitality of the early Church became but a memory. By about 500, the church had lost much of the essence of social holiness while continuing its empty forms of tradition and liturgy. Faith became institutionalized, hierarchical, and static. Under these conditions, faith dissipated. Christian faith was exercised in traditional forms, but diminished in reality. The exception to this in part was the social/spiritual life of monastic communities that emerged over time throughout Christendom.[53]

Christine Pohl writes that three institutional settings in the Middle Ages were important in reaching out to serve others in the practice of hospitality: monasteries and their hospices for pilgrims, hospitals, and the great ecclesial and lay households customarily for persons of higher status and wealth. However, such hospitality and care was not offered to all of one's neighbors.[54] In spite of an inclusive biblical admonition, only the wealthy and privileged received such benefit. The relief of the local poor, widows, orphans, and homeless was largely left to another age.

The Wesleys and the Methodists (1700-1900). When John Wesley and his brother Charles were in the early days of establishing Methodism as a renewal movement, the English religious establishment was in disarray and remained largely restricted to serving the upper classes of the wealthy. Wesley's theology of grace and full salvation was a departure from the norm. It reached out to the largely marginalized populous. In social holiness, these brothers recovered the ancient Christian practice of loving one's neighbor with encouragement, support, and accountability.

The practice of the small-group meetings of Methodism, the class, band, and society, were a means of "watching over one another in love." They promoted the spiritual formation and transformation of individual persons, but also of whole communities of faith, fueling a great awakening that reached out well beyond England. A new era of social holiness came into being as the Methodist movement grew with its promise of personal and social transformation.

Social Holiness in the Wesleyan Spirit

Throughout the nineteenth and twentieth centuries, out of the fecund soil of Wesleyan theology and practice, thousands of innovations in social holiness were birthed across five continents. Examples of the fruit of this social holiness include the following.

1. **The Anti-Slavery Movement.** In England the movement against slavery was led by William Wilberforce who was mentored by John Wesley. They helped inspire the fight against slavery in the United States in the mid-nineteenth century by Wesleyans, and in particular by Free Methodists under the leadership of B. T. Roberts. Both endeavors were social movements compelled by a collective movement of the Holy Spirit in a people called Methodists. Social holiness reached a critical level in both the UK and USA as a kind of leaven that nurtured virtuous hearts and minds that transformed popular will and led to the eventual abolition of slavery.

2. **The Preferential Option for the Poor.** George Allen Turner recalls that John Wesley professed and practiced the "great commandment" of Jesus (Matthew 22:38).

"During the earliest years at Oxford, care for the poor was prominent in the spiritual disciplines of the 'Holy Club'…. They [Methodists] took time to visit those in prison and to ride with convicts to the gallows with prayer for their eternal destinations…. In class meetings, a collection for the poor was regularly taken up." John Wesley believed that Methodism was a return to primitive Christianity and "took seriously the command to 'love thy neighbor' by giving to the poor and the orphan as well as ministering to prisoners." In so doing, Wesley was demonstrating and promoting a preferential option for reaching out to the poor.[55]

Urban Missions. In the context of social holiness in American Methodism, three sketches of social service to the poor are illustrative expressions of social holiness in Wesleyan urban mission.

a. **The Olive Branch Mission in South Chicago.** The Olive Branch Mission is not only the oldest rescue mission in Chicago, but also considered to be the oldest in the United States. The mission was started by Rachel Bradley as a sewing class for prostitutes in her church basement. Rachel sought an experience of sanctification at a Free Methodist camp meeting. In a subsequent prayer meeting in her Free Methodist church she was moved to open a mission for the poor. The sewing class grew into a mission, a place of safety and refuge on Wells Street for the homeless. It eventually moved to Chicago's "skid row." As a "light of the gospel" and a "spiritual oasis," the mission served and aided "destitute, fallen, and outcast" men and women. Many of the women had been forced by debt into prostitution, bought and sold, exploited in human sexual trafficking, inmates in the prisons of brothels. The Olive Branch Mission was truly a rescue mission in the spirit of social holiness.

b. **The Rest Cottage Mission in Cincinnati.** This mission was a work aimed in the urban slums. The founder of several missions was Seth Cook Rees, a minister and urban missionary. Jonathan Dodrill writes this about Rees' urban ministry: "He opened numerous rescue homes for the destitute: prostitutes, runaways, drunks and orphans.... Rees's preferential option for the poor was based on his pneumatology. He believed that the Spirit of God was giving special attention to the neglected and submerged classes."[56]

c. **Oakdale Christian Academy**, Jackson, Kentucky. Poverty may be found in settings other than in the slums of major cities. Wesleyan social holiness inspired educational innovation that reached out to the rural poor in Appalachia. Oakdale Academy was established as a residential school to educationally serve one of the poorest regions of the nation. It's current website reads: "Courage, perseverance, and faith are words that describe those who set out in 1921 to establish a Christian school in the heart of Appalachia. Elizabeth E. O'Connor started with a one-room elementary school for the children in the small community of Oakdale in southeastern Kentucky. As a mission of the Free Methodist

Church, the theological orientation of the academy was informed by Wesleyan-Arminian teaching, which calls for wholeness in personal, church, and civic life."

These three brief sketches exemplify the social holiness focus and communal commitment of hearts and minds of many Wesleyan Holiness denominations. They are a sample of Wesleyan social ecologies rendering service to others in fidelity to Jesus' great command to love others. It's the nature of gathered saints living together in social holiness to reach up to love God, to reach in for personal and communal strength and the wisdom of the Holy Spirit, and to relationally reach out to others with a healing touch, care, and compassion.

The magnitude of Wesleyan denominational initiatives today that reach out to persons who are poor, impoverished, marginalized, exploited, and disadvantaged is remarkable. The collective expressions of social and humanitarian service, inspired by the social holiness of Wesleyan faith communities around the world, is well beyond what John Wesley could have ever imagined.[57] Then there's the history of reaching out by The Salvation Army (the Army).

3. **The Salvation Army (1865).** The Salvation Army's mission statement is "to preach the gospel of Jesus Christ and to meet human needs in His name without discrimination." At the time of this writing, the Army is 152 years old and has had a global commitment to provide shelter to the poor, food to the hungry, clothes

to the naked, compassion to the sick, good news to those in prison, and a welcoming embrace to the alien, refugee, stranger, marginalized, and rejected, the "least of these" (Matthew 25:40).

The Army is described historically by Salvationist author Roger Green as waging a "war on two fronts."[58] The initial ministry and mission began with a solitary emphasis on redemption, preaching to and converting sinners. The founder, William Booth, began as an ordained clergyman in the Methodist New Connection and then in independent ministry to the poor in East London. In 1878 Booth changed the name of the ministry to The Salvation Army with the broadened mission of "getting saved and keeping saved, and then getting somebody else saved, and getting saved ourselves more and more, until full salvation on earth makes the heaven within, which is finally perfected by the full salvation without."

Up until 1880, Booth's war on sin and suffering was only on one front, spiritual salvation. Participants in the multi-national fight with Booth began to be aware that preaching the good news to the poor was not enough. It needed to be complimented with care for the physical needs of the poor. It's a fact that the Army's renowned social work among the poor did not begin with William Booth, but with the breaking out of innovations of compassionate social service in the subsequent years that soon followed in places like Melbourne, Australia (1883), Glasgow, Scotland (1884), and Toronto, Canada (1886). This was the beginning of the Army's war on two fronts that lead to a major shift in Booth's theology of redemption, the publication of his book, *Darkest England and the Way*

Out (1890),[59] and the Army's full embrace of both personal and social salvation.

The Army is often best known for reaching out to serve suffering humanity. Its reaching out is done through the ministry of residential hostels for the homeless, emergency lodges, children's homes, homes for the elderly, the disabled and blind, for street children and abandoned babies, residential care homes/hostels, day care centers, residential and non-residential addiction programs, Harbor Light centers for alcohol recovery, services to the armed forces, emergency disaster response programs, prison ministries, missing persons bureaus, emergency relief (fire, flood, etc.), hostels for students, general hospitals, hospice centers, health education programs, community centers, and over 3,000 schools (primary, kindergarten, middle, secondary, vocational, colleges and universities).[60]

The global extent of the Army's programs and social services, relative to its modest size, is a reality only explained as the grace of God. In the context of its humanity (collective shortcomings, flaws, and weaknesses), God's grace remains sufficient. The totality of its efforts to actively integrate faith with service, reaching out to others with the love of Jesus, does not in itself constitute social holiness. However, the work of the Army in 128 countries and 176 languages is pursued in continual, unified fidelity to its doctrine of holiness and its practice of self-giving, self-sacrificing love of God and others.

The overarching idea of the Army, as an integral part of the larger Body of Christ, is found in its identity and mission. The Army is a means of grace compelled by the Trinitarian love of God. It continues to reach out to vulnerable others, in solidarity with other Wesleyan Holiness communities of faith around the world, animated in social holiness to the praise of God's glory.

DISCUSSION QUESTIONS

1. In what ways do you "let your light shine" in social holiness by reaching out to others and how might that bring glory to God?

2. How might the influence and presence of others help you to reach up to God, go deeper in holiness, and reach out more to others?

3. As the gospel has come to you through others, how do you work with others to pass it on?

4. Whose company do you now keep that makes it possible to serve God and others in ways that exceed what you might do on your own?

fourteen

EPILOGUE

Testimony and Thesis

Go make disciples.

Matthew 28:18

This discussion of social holiness reflects a personal testimony. My witness is simple. My faith was established with the help of others. Yet faith can dissipate when, in social contexts outside the sanctified company of others, we forget the presence and company of God. At one time in such a state, I ceased to engage the means by which I could stay in close proximity and contact with God. Nevertheless, God's provision included the company of others, friends and mentors, authors, co-workers, exemplars, and family.

Looking back over the years, I can see how Scripture provided wisdom and understanding about these things. Jesus clarified the importance of remaining in his company, remaining in him and with his other disciples. The writings of the Paul encourage us to continue in Christ, rooted and built up, established in the

Kingdom, grasping the magnitude of God's love, and filled to the measure of the fullness of God. God's words through Jeremiah warn about being a people who do not listen and find themselves in ruinous, spiritually toxic conditions. Environments that lack Spirit-based nutrients lead to a kind of spiritual malnourishment, a diminished spiritual well-being, and a dissipation of faith. That was my story at a formative time in my life.

My testimony includes reflection on my encounter with holy discontent over my drift of faith away from God. By sheer grace, God brought an author, E. Stanley Jones, into my life. His devotional book *The Word Became Flesh*[61] mentored me back to the loving company of the "Other," Jesus Christ, my Lord and Savior. I stepped back into the zone of others who helped me maintain an awareness of God's presence and unfailing love. I began to recognize and respond to God's grace in my life.

I returned to my former life with the company of saints and knowing God in ever-increasing intimacy. My holy discontent was no longer guilt over my neglect of God. Instead, holy discontent was from a deep yearning for more. I desired to grasp the fullness of God's immeasurable love, His presence and power to love Him and others, and to do so profoundly. What was true in Scripture and my personal experience made increasing sense when viewed through the lenses of social psychology and the social/spiritual ecology of human development.

Since childhood, I've resonated with the idea that God the Potter had His hands on the clay of my life, shaping me into something of value. It was only later that I came to understand that God does that for us through human agency, the loving company of others. God engages others in the process of our full salvation. It's in their presence that God's presence and identity become known. God reveals Himself and does so in many ways, especially through the faithfulness of others. It was only later that I came to see that we are those "others" living for and serving others, those who are all along George Barna's transformational "stops." Together, we are the Potter's wheels in the spiritual formation of others. We are privileged partners in God's divine plan of Creation healed. Praise God!

All holiness is social holiness. Others are central to God's means of grace, powerful presence, and plan for full salvation in the healing of all creation. The gospel comes and is passed on through the salvific context of sanctifying relationships. The full gospel is the complete redemptive, reconciling, restorative, glorifying message of God's Word and work in the world. It proclaims and reveals the divine presence and identity, mission and plan for our salvation and that of all creation.

Our engagement in God's salvation of others is our unimaginable privilege to be participants with God in making disciples, saints who become mature and sanctified. As saints in God's company and in that of others, we grow and go on to serve in ways that contribute to the God's Kingdom now and yet to come. We do this for the ultimate *telos*, the praise of God's glory!

The Thesis of Social Holiness

In the Garden of Gethsemane before his arrest, Jesus prayed for his disciples (John 17:20-23). We see there his triple *telos* for the disciples. His prayer was that they be one... that the world may believe...that the world may know. They had been in his company for three or so years and he desired them to be sanctified wholly and in unity with him and the Father by the Spirit. That last night in the garden, Christ prayed to the Father, "Sanctify them by the truth; your word is truth.... I sanctify myself that they too may be truly sanctified." Then he expanded his vision of discipleship and growing saints by praying for all believers, including us yet to come:

> My prayer is not for them [his first disciples] alone.
> I pray for those who will believe in me through their

message, that all of them may be one, Father, just as you are in me and I am in you, may they also be in us so that the world may believe that you sent me. I have given them the glory that you gave me, that they may be one as we are one: I in them and you in me. May they be brought to complete unity to let the world know that you sent me and have loved them even as you have loved me (John 17:20-23).

Jesus' prayer to the Father is the thesis of this book. Ultimately, social holiness is a relational context (ecology) of complete fulfillment when, in the company we keep, we become one with the one God who is perfect in unity within the Godhead, Father, Son, and Holy Spirit. Our Father passed on the Word, Jesus Christ his Son, who passed on himself by the Holy Spirit to his disciples and to the world, so that the fullness of God's salvation would be made possible for all humankind. As holiness comes to us, it is to be passed on to others through our dying to self and rising to follow Jesus.

The presence and love of Jesus for us was real in the past before we knew he existed. We came to know of his presence and love because of the love of other saints in the social contexts of family, friends, church, work, media, and other settings in which the Holy Spirit was at work. The company of other saints made it real for us. The gospel came to us by the Word and the Spirit through them. In obedience, they helped make real Christ's presence and love.

Along with the Father through the Holy Spirit, Jesus Christ remains faithful as his essence in us purifies us and makes us one with God. He makes our unity with God possible so that we may participate in God's divine social nature as we pass on His holy love to others. This is the nature of social holiness through the company we keep. Thanks be to God! Glory be to God!

DISCUSSION QUESTIONS

1. What's your testimony? How balanced and overlapping are your three areas of head, heart, and life (knowing, loving, and living Christ)?

2. In the center where the three areas overlap, are you growing in unity with and likeness to God?

3. If you become the company you keep, describe the people who are your present company, your social/spiritual ecology.

4. Are you now filled with the fullness of God in holiness and purity of heart?

5. Is God now doing immeasurably more in and through your life so that you have profound love for God and profound love for others?

6. Do you feel like you are a guest at the table of the Holy Trinity and that your prayer life is the Trinity inviting you into the conversation of the Trinity?

ENDNOTES

1   "Minutes of Several Conversations, Q.3." In *The Works of John Wesley*, edited by Thomas Jackson, 299. Grand Rapids, Michigan: Baker Books, 1978.

2   *The Works of John Wesley.* Vol. 14, 321. Grand Rapids, Michigan: Baker Books, 2002.

3   Rohr, Richard, and Mike Morrell. *The Divine Dance: The Trinity and Your Transformation.* New Kensington, PA: Whitaker House, 2016, 29-30. See also Seamand, Stephen. *Ministry in the Image of God: The trinitarian shape of christian service.* Grand Rapids: InterVarsity Press, 2005.

4   "Hymns and Sacred Poems (1739), Preface Chapter 5." In *The Works of John Wesley*, by John Wesley, 321. Grand Rapids, Michigan: Baker Books, 2002.

5   Wesley, John. "Upon Our Lord's Sermon on the Mount IV (1748)." In *John Wesley's Sermons: An anthology*, edited by Albert Outler and R. Heitzenrater, 195-196. Nashville, TN: Abingdon Press, 1987.

6   Wesley, John. "The More Excellent Way, Sermon 89, 1787." In *John Wesley's Sermons: An anthology*, edited by Albert C. Outler and

Richard P. Heitzenrater, 195-196. Nashville, Tennessee: Abingdon Press, 1991.

7   Turner, George Allen. *The More Excellent Way: Scriptural Basis of the Wesleyan Message.* Winona Lake: Light & Life Press, 1958.

8   Leclerc, Diane. *Discovering Christian Holiness: The Heart of Wesleyan-holiness Theology, 59.* Kansas City: Beacon Hill Press, 2010.

9   Brengle, Samuel Logan. *The Way of Holiness, 4.* Atlanta, Georgia: The Salvation Army, 1980. Commissioner Brengle was a prolific author and proponent of the Wesleyan doctrine of holiness whose works also included *Helps to Holiness, The Heart of Holiness, Come Holy Guest,* and *Heart Talks on Holiness.* For a complete discourse on Brengle, see Rightmire, David R. *Santified Sanity: The Life and Teaching of Samuel Logan Brengle.* Revised and Expanded Edition. Wilmore, Kentucky: Francis Asbury Society, 2014.

10   Green, Roger. "What is Holiness." In *The Holiness Manifesto,* 234, edited by Kevin Mannoia and Don Thorsen, 2008. Grand Rapids, Michigan: William B. Eerdmans Publishing Co., 2008. Roger Green, Lyell Rader and I were appointed by The Salvation Army as original members of the Wesleyan Holiness Study Group in 2003 when it was first formed as the forerunner to the current Wesleyan Holiness Connection. The book *Holiness Manifesto* was one of the tangible outcomes of the study group's work and contains a rich array of papers by twenty-one authors from holiness heritage universities and seminaries and eight Wesleyan holiness denominations. For more information on the Wesleyan Holiness Connection, please visit www.holinessandunity.org.

11   Coutts, Frederick. *The Call to Holiness, 107.* St. Albans: The Campfield Press, 1957.

12   Watson, Kevin M. *The Class Meeting.* Franklin, Tennessee: Seedbed Publishing, 2014, 46-47. See also Runyon, Theodore. *The New Creation: John Wesley's Theology Today.* Nashville, Tennessee: Abingdon Press, 1998, 27. Also see Watson, Kevin M. *Pursuing Social Holiness: The Band Meeting in Wesley's Thought and Popular Methodist Practice.* New York, New York: Oxford University Press, 2014. A more recent and more extensive treatment of the topic.

13   Wesley, John. "The Scripture Way of Salvation." In *John Wesley's Sermons: An Anthology*, edited by Albert C, 374. Outler and Richard P. Heitzenrater. Nashville, Tennessee: Abingdon Press, 1991.

14   When a good friend proofread this book as a first draft, she shared another version of the house analogy of holiness. She said, "We are the house; in salvation, God moves in, begins his work in various rooms; eventually we turn over the deed to him; our 'all' become his." Moulton, Yvonne. *Editorial Notes/ Comments from Social Holiness: The Company We Keep* Wilmore, Kentucky, (March 2017): Ch. 5 - In the Zone.

15   Barna, George. *Maximum Faith: Live Like Jesus.* Ventura: Metaformation, Inc., Ventura, California/ Stratagenius Group, LLC, New York, New York/ Wesleyan Holiness Consortium Publishing, Glendora, California, 2011.

16   Doing good and being busy in church activity is not the problem. Rather, the concern is activity that engages only in social life and leads to spiritual stasis. Activities that serve the Kingdom and grow saints are too often not a priority nor are there forms of support and accountability that insure fidelity to Kingdom concerns.

17   Walt, J. D. "The Whole Gospel: Getting on with the Second Half of Salvation." In *Seedbed Sower's Almanac and Seed Catalog*, edited by J. D. Walt and Andrew Miller, 32-34. Franklin, Tennessee: Seedbed Publishing, 2015.

18   Walt, J. D. "The Problem with Growing Churches." In *Seedbed Sower's Almanac and Seed Catalog*, edited by J. D. Walt, 36-39. Franklin, Tennessee: Seedbed Publishing, 2016.

19   Newbigin, Lesslie. *The Open Secret: An Introduction to the Theology of Mission*, 125. Revised Edition. Grand Rapids, Michigan: Eerdmans, 1978. Here J. D. Walt echoes Lesslie Newbigin. "Neither does a study of the Epistle seem to disclose any interest in numerical growth. We do not find Paul concerning himself with the size of the churches or with questions about their growth. His primary concern is with their faithfulness, with the integrity of the witness.... There is a deep concern for the integrity of the Christian witness, but there is no

evidence of anxiety about or enthusiasm for rapid growth. In no sense does the triumph of God's reign seem to depend upon the growth of the church."

20   Gowans, John. *General John Gowans: 'We Are Here To Save Souls, To Grow Saints and To Serve Suffering Humanity'*. Ann. September 23, 2013. http://fitformission.salvationarmy.org.uk/general-john-gowans-we-are-here-save-souls-grow-saints-and-serve-suffering-humanity (accessed September 13, 2017). In 1999, John Gowans was elected to the position of General as the international leader of The Salvation Army. On that occasion he was interviewed by the *Salvationist* and asked "What can we quietly and cheerfully discard and what must we keep at any price?" He answered, "The Salvation Army was created to achieve three very definite things. It was created to save souls, to grow saints, and to serve suffering humanity. If we stop doing any one of those three, The Salvation Army will cease to be The Salvation Army."

21   Wesley, John. *On Dissipation, Sermon 79 - The Sermons of John Wesley*. Edited by Michael Anderson, Ryan Danker and George Lyons. Wesley Center for Applied Theology at Northwest Nazarene University. 1999. http://wesley.nnu.edu/john-wesley/the-sermons-of-john-wesley-1872-edition/sermon-79-on-dissipation/ (accessed September 13, 2017).

22   Wesley, John. "Wesley to Wilberforce: John Wesley's Last Letter from his Deathbed." *Christian History*, 1983.

23   Mandela, Nelson. *Long Walk to Freedom: Autobiography*. Boston, Massachusetts: Little Brown & Co., 1995. This autobiography by former South African President Nelson Mandela profiles his life. In particular, it gives insight into his early life, coming of age, education in the Methodist church's educational system from grade one throughout his college days, residence in the Wesley residence hall while in law school, and twenty-seven years of reflection in prison.

24   Newcomb, Theodore M. *The Acquaintance Process*, 3. New York: Holt, Rinehart and Winston, 1961.

25   Baillargeon, Renee. "Object Permanence in 3 1/2- and 4 1/2-Month-Old Infants." *Developmental Psychology* (American Psychological Association, Inc.) 23, no. 5 (1987): 655-664.

26   Warneken, F., and M. Tomasello. "Altruistic Helping in Human Infants and Young Chimpanzees." *Science* 311, no. 5765 (2006): 1301-1303.

27   Ross, Lee, Mark Lepper, and Andrew Ward. *History of Social Psychology: Insights, Challenges, and Contributions to the Theory and Application.* Vol. 1, in *Handbook of Social Psychology*, edited by Susan T. Fiske, Daniel T. Gilber and Gardner Lindzey, 3-50. Hoboken, New Jersey: John Wiley & Sons, Inc., 2009.

28   Hill, Craig A. "Ways, Affiliation Motivation: People Who Need People." *Journal of Personality and Social Psychology* 52, no. 5 (1987): 1008-1018.

29   Snyder, Howard. *Personal Communication.* Wilmore, Kentucky (March 2017). "Yes, yet God is holiness and also requires obedience, purity, and renunciation of sin."

30   Clark, Margaret S., and Edward P. Lemay. *Close Relationships.* Vol. 2, in *Handbook of Social Psychology*, edited by Susan T. Fiske, Daniel T. Gilbert and Gardner Lindzey, 898-940. Hoboken, New Jersey: John Wiley & Sons, Inc., 2009.

31   Callen, Barry L., ed. *The Holy River of God: Currents and Contributions of the Wesleyan Holiness Stream of Christianity.* Spring Valley: Aldersgate Press, 2016. This source presents a comprehensive account.

32   Leclerc, Diane. *Discovering Christian Holiness: The Heart of Wesleyan-holiness Theology*, 264. Kansas City: Beacon Hill Press, 2010.

33   John Wesley considered the Eucharist to be a means of grace and took a position of permitting, if not encouraging, non-believers to participate in the belief that by so doing some would come to faith in Jesus Christ. The Salvation Army's initial pragmatic, non-sacramental practice continues to be a conundrum for many in its departure from all other Wesleyan holiness denominations. It is viewed as a subordination of ecclesiology to pneumatology necessitating a reevaluation of its sacramental theology and encouragement to by others for the Army to return to a truly Wesleyan appreciation of entire sanctification, engaging both process and crisis. In response to this concern, Rightmire, David. The Sacramental Journey of the Salvation Army: A Study of Holiness Foundations. 2nd, 268. Alexandria, Virginia: Crest Books/

Booklocker.com, Inc., 2016, writes, "In this light, it may be prudent to remember the words of the Founder, as recorded in his 1883 "New Years Address to Officers," in which he announced his decision to discontinue observance of the sacraments… 'is it not wise for us to postpone any settlement of the [sacramental] question, to leave over to some future day, when we shall have more light, and see more clearly our way before us.'"

34   Back, M.D., S.C. Schmukle, and B. Egloff. "Becoming Friends by Chance." *Psychological Sciences*, 2008: 439-440. See also Festinger, Leon, Kurt W. Back, and Stanley Schachter. *Social Pressures in Informal Groups: A Study of Human Factors in Housing*. Palo Alto, California: Standford University Press, 1950. Johnson, Martin A. "Variables Associated with Friendship in an Adult Population." *Journal of Social Psychology* 129, no. 3 (1989): 379-390.

35   Bornstein, Robert F. "Exposure and Affect: Overview and Meta-analysis of Research, 1968–1987." Edited by Dolores Albarracín. *Psychological Bulletin* (American Psychological Association) 106, no. 2 (September 1989): 265-289.

36   Raymond, Jonathan S. "Our Cascading Doctrines." Edited by Roger Green and Jonathan Raymond. *Word & Deed: The Salvation Army Journal of Theology and Ministry* 17, no. 2 (2015).

37   Watson, David L. *The Early Methodist Class Meeting: Its Origins and Significance*, 94. Eugene: Wipf and Stock Publishers, 1985.

38   At the time I was an adjunct professor in the department of psychology and a clinical professor of medicine at the University of Hawaii while serving as the chief administrator of The Salvation Army's (TSA) Addiction Treatment Facilities (ATF). The ATF was a small system of seven programs of mental health, drug and alcohol abuse treatment funded by the Hawaii State Department of Health. Women's Way was part of TSA system begun then as a cutting-edge program diverting women out of the criminal justice system into treatment with their children. More than a social service, it became a social ecology of health, wholeness, and spiritual formation. It still is operating after nearly forty years.

39   Kinlaw, Dennis F. *Let's Start with Jesus: A new way of doing theology*, 52-56. Grand Rapids, Michigan: Zondervan, 2005.

40   Raymond, Jonathan S. *Higher Higher Education: Integrating holiness into all of campus life.* Spring Valley: Aldersgate Press, 2015. This is an extensive discussion of the social/ spiritual contexts of universities and colleges that can promote holiness as as student outcome.

41   Collins, Kenneth, interview by Jonathan S. Raymond. *Personal Communication.* Asbury University. Professor of Historical Theology & Wesley Studies, Wilmore. n.d. See also Diane Leclerc's definition of synergism. Leclerc, Diane. *Discovering Christian Holiness: The Heart of Wesleyan-holiness Theology*, 319. Kansas City: Beacon Hill Press, 2010.

42   Needham, Phil. *When God Becomes Small.* Nashville: Abingdon Press, 2014.

43   *The Salvation Army Handbook of Doctrine.* London: Salvation Books: The Salvation Army International Headquarters, 2010.

44   Bronfenbrenner, Urie. *The Ecology of Human Development: Experiments by Nature and Design*, 13. Cambridge: Harvard University Press, 1979.

45   Knight, III., Henry H. *The Presence of God in the Christian Life: John Wesley and the Means of Grace.* Oxford: Scarecrow Press, 1992.

46   Stott, John R.W. *The Spirit the Church and the World: The message of Acts.* Downers Grove, Illinois: Intervarsity Press, 1990. In his original commentary, Stott portrays Luke's work as not so much the "Acts of the Apostles" but as the continuing work of Jesus Christ by the Spirit, through the church, to the world.

47   See God's earth covenant, Genesis 9:1-17.

48   Snyder, Howard A., and Joel Scandrett. *Salvation Means Creation Healed: The Ecology of Sin and Grace: Overcoming the divorce between earth and heaven.* Eugene, Oregon: Cascade Books: an imprint of Wipf and Stock Publishers, 2011. I am indebted to Howard Snyder, a friend and by his writings a mentor, whose discussion in this particular work has influenced my thinking about sin, salvation, and *telos* in the writing of chapter twelve and in his general comments on the text as its writing progressed.

49   Needham, Phil. *Community in Mission: A salvationist ecclesiology*, 75-90. London, United Kingdom: The Salvation Army International Headquarters, 1987.

50   Hellerman, Joseph H. *When the Church Was a Family: Recapturing Jesus' vision for authentic Christian community*, 79-82, 85-89. Nashville, Tennessee: B&H Publishing Group, 2009. This is a robust discussion of the affective and material solidarity of the early church.

51   Dieter, Melvin E. "The Wesleyan Perspective." In *Five Views on Sanctification*, 13, by Melvin E. Dieter, Anthony A. Hoekema, Stanley M. Horton, J. Robertson McQuilkin and John F. Walvoord, edited by Stanley N. Gundry, 13. Grand Rapids, Michigan: Zondervan, 1987.

52   Hellerman, Joseph H. *When the Church Was a Family: Recapturing Jesus' vision for authentic Christian community*, 119. Nashville, Tennessee: B&H Publishing Group, 2009.

53   Oden, Thomas C. *How Africa Shaped the Christian Mind: Rediscovering the African seedbed of western Christianity*. Downers Grove, Illinois: InterVarsity Press, 2010. This is an extensive review of the matter.

54   Pohl, Christine D. *Making Room: Recovering hospitality as a Christian tradition*, 48-50. Grand Rapids: Wm. B. Eerdmans Publishing Co., 1999.

55   Turner, George Allen. *Churches of the Restoration: A study in origins*, 135-136. Lewiston, New York: Edwin Mellen Press, 1994.

56   Dodrill, Jonathan. "Kenosis Not Control: The social holiness of Chicago's urban missions." In *Holy Imagination: Rethinking Social Holiness*, edited by Nathan Crawford, Jonathan Dodrill and David Wilson, 62-71. Lexington, Kentucky: Emeth Press, 2015.

57   Callen, Barry L., ed. *The Holy River of God: Currents and Contributions of the Wesleyan Holiness Stream of Christianity*. Spring Valley: Aldersgate Press, 2016. This provides an excellent discussion of Wesleyan Holiness denominations reaching out.

58   Green, Roger. *War on Two Fronts: The redemptive theology of William Booth*, 78. Alexandria, Virginia: Crest Books, 2017.

59   Booth, William. *In Darkest England and the Way Out.* London, United
        Kingdom: The Salvation Army, 1890.

60   The Salvation Army International Headquarters. *The Salvation Army
        Year Book 2016.* London, United Kingdom: The Salvation Army
        International Headquarters, 2015.

61   Jones, E. Stanley. *The Word Became Flesh.* Nashville, Tennessee:
        Abingdon Press, 1963.

BIBLIOGRAPHY

Baby Center, L.L.C. (2017). *How to Change a Disposable Diaper*. Retrieved from Baby Center: http://www.babycenter.com/0_how-to-change-a-disposable-diaper_3838.bc

Back, M., Schmukle, S., & Egloff, B. (2008). Becoming Friends by Chance. *Psychological Sciences*, 439-440.

Baillargeon, R. (1987). Object Permanence in 3 1/2- and 4 1/2-Month-Old Infants. *Developmental Psychology, 23*(5), 655-664. Retrieved from http://internal.psychology.illinois.edu/infantlab/articles/baillargeon 1987.pdf.pdf

Barna, G. (2011). *Maximum Faith: Live Like Jesus*. Ventura: Metaformation, Inc., Ventura, California/ Stratagenius Group, LLC, New York, New York/ Wesleyan Holiness Consortium Publishing, Glendora, California.

Booth, W. (1890). *In Darkest England and the Way Out*. London, United Kingdom: The Salvation Army.

Bornstein, R. F. (1989, September). Exposure and affect: Overview and meta-analysis of research, 1968–1987. (D. Albarracín, Ed.) *Psychological Bulletin, 106*(2), 265-289.

Brengle, S. L. (1980). *The Way of Holiness*. Atlanta, Georgia: The Salvation Army.

Bronfenbrenner, U. (1979). *The Ecology of Human Development: Experiments by nature and design*. Cambridge: Harvard University Press.

Callen, B. L. (Ed.). (2016). *The Holy River of God: Currents and Contributions of the Wesleyan Holiness Stream of Christianity*. Spring Valley: Aldersgate Press.

Clark, M. S., & Lemay, E. P. (2009). Close Relationships. In S. T. Fiske, D. T. Gilbert, & G. Lindzey (Eds.), *Handbook of Social Psychology* (Vol. 2, pp. 898-940). Hoboken, New Jersey: John Wiley & Sons, Inc.

Collins, K. (n.d.). Personal Communication. (J. S. Raymond, Interviewer) Asbury University. Professor of Historical Theology & Wesley Studies, Wilmore.

Coutts, F. (1957). *The Call to Holiness*. St. Albans: The Campfield Press.

Dieter, M. E. (1987). The Wesleyan Perspective. In M. E. Dieter, A. A. Hoekema, S. M. Horton, J. R. McQuilkin, J. F. Walvoord, & S. N. Gundry (Ed.), *Five Views on Sanctification* (p. 13). Grand Rapids, Michigan: Zondervan.

Dodrill, J. (2015). Kenosis Not Control: The social holiness of Chicago's urban missions. In N. Crawford, J. Dodrill, & D. Wilson (Eds.), *Holy Imagination: Rethinking social holiness* (pp. 62-71). Lexington, Kentucky: Emeth Press.

Engle, P. E., & Spohrer, J. A. (2003). *Serving in Your Church Nursery: Zondervan Practical Ministry Guide (Nursery)*. Grand Rapids: Zondervan.

Festinger, L., Back, K. W., & Schachter, S. (1950). *Social Pressures in Informal Groups: A Study of Human Factors in Housing*. Palo Alto, California: Standford University Press.

Gowans, J. (2013, September 23). *General John Gowans: 'We Are Here To Save Souls, To Grow Saints And To Serve Suffering Humanity'*. (Ann, Producer, & The Salvation Army UK Territory with the Republic of Ireland, Territorial Headquarters) Retrieved September 13, 2017, from Fit for Mission: http://fitformission.salvationarmy.org.uk/general-john-gowans-we-are-here-save-souls-grow-saints-and-serve-suffering-humanity

Green, R. (2008). What is Holiness. In K. Mannoia, & D. Thorsen (Eds.), *The Holiness Manifesto* (p. 2008). Grand Rapids, Michigan: William B. Eerdmans Publishing Co.

Green, R. (2017). *War on Two Fronts: The redemptive theology of William Booth.* Alexandria, Virginia: Crest Books.

Hellerman, J. H. (2009). *When the Church Was a Family: Recapturing Jesus' vision for authentic Christian community.* Nashville, Tennessee: B&H Publishing Group.

Hill, C. A. (1987). Ways, Affiliation Motivation: People Who Need People... But in Different. *Journal of Personality and Social Psychology, 52*(5), 1008-1018. Retrieved from https://www.researchgate.net/publication/19575626_ Affiliation_Motivation_People_Who_Need_People_But_in_ Different_Ways

Hinzman, S. (2017, June 02). *VBS Finale - CAMEO Night - LemonAIDe Finale.* Lexington, Kentucky: The Salvation Army Eastern Territory.

Hymns and Sacred Poems (1739), Preface Chapter 5. (2002). In J. Wesley, *The Works of John Wesley* (p. 321). Grand Rapids, Michigan: Baker Books.

Johnson, M. A. (1989). Variables Associated with Friendship in an Adult Population. *Journal of Social Psychology, 129*(3), 379-390.

Jones, E. S. (1963). *The Word Became Flesh.* Nashville, Tennessee: Abingdon Press.

Kinlaw, D. F. (2005). *Let's Start with Jesus: A new way of doing theology.* Grand Rapids, Michigan: Zondervan.

Knight, III., H. H. (1992). *The Presence of God in the Christian Life: John Wesley and the means of grace.* Oxford: Scarecrow press.

Leclerc, D. (2010). *Discovering Christian Holiness: The heart of Wesleyan-holiness theology.* Kansas City: Beacon Hill Press.

Mandela, N. (1995). *Long Walk to Freedom: Autobiography.* Boston, Massachusetts: Little Brown & Co.

McGavran. (1974). The Dimensions of World Evangelization. *International Congress on World Evangelization* (pp. 108-115). Lausanne: Lausanne 1974 Documents. Retrieved from https://www.lausanne.org/wp-content/uploads/2007/06/0108.pdf

Minutes of Several Conversations, Q.3. (1978). In T. Jackson (Ed.), *The Works of John Wesley* (p. 299). Grand Rapids, Michigan: Baker Books.

Moulton, Y. (2017, March). Editorial Notes/ Comments from Social Holiness: The Company We Keep. Ch. 5 - In the Zone. Wilmore, Kentucky.

Needham, P. (1987). *Community in Mission: A salvationist ecclesiology.* London, United Kingdom: The Salvation Army International Headquarters.

Needham, P. (2014). *When God Becomes Small.* Nashville: Abingdon Press.

Newbigin, L. (1978). *The Open Secret: An Introduction to the Theology of Mission* (Revised Edition ed.). Grand Rapids, Michigan: Eerdmans.

Newcomb, T. M. (1961). *The Acquaintance Process.* New York: Holt, Rinehart and Winston.

Oden, T. C. (2010). *How Africa Shaped the Christian Mind: Rediscovering the African seedbed of western Christianity.* Downers Grove, Illinois: InterVarsity Press.

Orange Curriculum. (2017). *First Look Pre-K Curriculum.* Retrieved from Orange: http://www.thinkorange.com/firstlook

Parlakian, R., & Lerner, C. (2008). *Your Baby's Development 3-6 Months.* Retrieved from Zero to Three: https://www.zerotothree.org/document/46

Pohl, C. D. (1999). *Making Room: Recovering hospitality as a Christian tradition.* Grand Rapids: Wm. B. Eerdmans Publishing Co.

Pronfenbrenner, U. (1979). *The Ecology of Human Development: Experiments by nature and design.* Cambridge: Harvard University Press.

Raymond, J. S. (2015). *Higher Higher Education: Integrating holiness into all of campus life.* Spring Valley: Aldersgate Press.

Raymond, J. S. (2015). Our Cascading Doctrine. (R. Green, & J. Raymond, Eds.) *Word & Deed: The Salvation Army Journal of Theology and Ministry, 17*(2).

Rightmire, D. R. (2014). *Sanctified Sanity: The life and teaching of Samuel Logan Brengle* (Revised and Expanded Edition ed.). Wilmore, Kentucky: Francis Asbury Society.

Rightmire, D. R. (2016). *The Sacramental Journey of the Salvation Army: A Study of Holiness Foundations* (2nd ed.). Alexandria, Virginia: Crest Books/ Booklocker.com, Inc.

Rohr, R., & Morrell, M. (2016). *The Divine Dance: The Trinity and Your Transformation.* New Kensington, PA: Whitaker House.

Ross, L., Lepper, M., & Ward, A. (2009). History of Social Psychology: Insights, Challenges, and Contributions to the Theory and Application. In S. T. Fiske, D. T. Gilber, & G. Lindzey (Eds.), *Handbook of Social Psychology* (Vol. 1, pp. 3-50). Hoboken, New Jersey: John Wiley & Sons, Inc.

Runyon, T. (1998). *The New Creation: John Wesley's Theology Today.* Nashville, Tennessee: Abingdon Press.

Seamand, S. (2005). *Ministry in the Image of God: The trinitarian shape of Christian service.* Grand Rapids: InterVarsity Press.

Snyder, H. (2017, March). Personal Communication. Wilmore, Kentucky.

Snyder, H. A., & Scandrett, J. (2011). *Salvation Means Creation Healed: The ecology of sin and grace: Overcoming the divorce between earth and heaven.* Eugene, Oregon: Cascade Books: an imprint of Wipf and Stock Publishers.

Stott, J. R. (1990). *The Spirit the Church and the World: The message of Acts.* Downers Grove, Illinois: Intervarsity Press.

The Salvation Army Handbook of Doctrine. (2010). London, United Kingdom: Salvation Books: The Salvation Army International Headquarters.

The Salvation Army International Headquarters. (2015). *The Salvation Army Year Book 2016.* London, United Kingdom: The Salvation Army International Headquarters.

Turner, G. A. (1958). *The More Excellent Way: Scriptural Basis of the Wesleyan Message.* Winona Lake: Light & Life Press.

Turner, G. A. (1994). *Churches of the Restoration: A study in origins.* Lewiston, New York: Edwin Mellen Press.

Walt, J. (2015). The Whole Gospel: Getting on with the Second Half of Salvation. In J. Walt, & A. Miller (Eds.), *Seedbed Sower's Almanac and Seed Catalog* (pp. 32-34). Franklin, Tennessee: Seedbed Publishing.

Walt, J. (2016). The Problem with Growing Churches. In J. Walt (Ed.), *Seedbed Sower's Almanac and Seed Catalog* (pp. 36-39). Franklin, Tennessee: Seedbed Publishing.

Warneken, F., & Tomasello, M. (2006). Altruistic Helping in Human Infants and Young Chimpanzees. *Science, 311*(5765), 1301-1303.

Warner, L. (2008, Spring). Spreading Scriptural Holiness: Theology and Practices of Early Methodism for the Contemporary Church. (T. C. Muck, Ed.) *The Asbury Journal, 63*(1), 115-138.

Watson, D. L. (1985). *The Early Methodist Class Meeting: Its origins and significance.* Eugene: Wipf and Stock Publishers.

Watson, K. M. (2014). *Pursuing Social Holiness: The Band Meeting in Wesley's Thought and Popular Methodist Practice.* New York, New York: Oxford University Press.

Watson, K. M. (2014). *The Class Meeting.* Franklin, Tennessee: Seedbed Publishing.

Wesley, J. (1983). Wesley to Wilberforce: John Wesley's Last Letter from his Deathbed. *Christian History*(2). Retrieved from www.christian historyinstitute.org/uploaded/50b77f4ed6bbc7.29263299.pdf

Wesley, J. (1987). Upon Our Lord's Sermon on the Mount IV (1748). In A. Outler, & R. Heitzenrater (Eds.), *John Wesley's Sermons: An anthology* (pp. 195-196). Nashville, TN: Abingdon Press.

Wesley, J. (1991). The More Excellent Way, Sermon 89, 1787. In A. C. Outler, & R. P. Heitzenrater (Eds.), *John Wesley's Sermons: An anthology* (pp. 195-196). Nashville, Tennessee: Abingdon Press.

Wesley, J. (1991). The Scripture Way of Salvation. In A. C. Outler, & R. P. Heitzenrater (Eds.), *John Wesley's Sermons: An anthology* (p. 374). Nashville, Tennessee: Abingdon Press.

Wesley, J. (1999). *On Dissipation, Sermon 79 - The Sermons of John Wesley.* (M. Anderson, R. Danker, G. Lyons, Editors, & Wesley Center for Applied Theology at Northwest Nazarene University) Retrieved September 13, 2017, from Wesley Center Online: http://wesley.nnu.edu/john-wesley/ the-sermons-of-john-wesley-1872-edition/sermon-79-on-dissipation/

Wesley, J. (2002). *The Works of John Wesley* (Vol. 14). Grand Rapids, Michigan: Baker Books.

Zajonc, R. B. (1968). Attitudinal effects of mere exposure. (K. Kawakami, & M. L. Cooper, Eds.) *Journal of Personality and Social Psychology, 9*(2, Pt. 2), 1-27.